Voice of the Trumpetess

MAE AZANGO

Forte Publishing

First Published in 2017
Published by:

FORTE Publications
#12 Ashmun Street
Snapper Hill
Monrovia, Liberia
[+231] 777155-923
[+231] 881-106-177

FORTE Publishing
7202 Tavenner Lane
208 Alexandria
VA, 22306

FORTE Press
76 Sarasit Road
Ban Pong, 70110
Ratchaburi, Thailand
[+66] 85-824-4382

http://fortepublishing.wix.com/fppp
fortepublishing@gmaill.com

Printed in the United States of America

ISBN: 0994630840
ISBN-13: 978-0994630841

DEDICATION

To the Loving Memories of my Parents,
Robert G.W. Azango and Bertha Baker Azango
my fiery Aunt, Grace L. Morris
and Sarah Carter, my Grandmother.

For all those who died in the Liberian Wars

CONTENT

ACKNOWLEDGMENTS

Many people played some part in this project, way too many to name here. However, I hope you understand that your efforts are appreciated, named or not.

There are few whose role deserve mention:

My Godmother and proofreader, Prof. Lorraine Schmall; my fearless publisher, Mr. Rodney Sieh; my New Narratives boss, Mrs. Prue Clarke; my darling big sister, Mrs. Lovette Azango Tucker; my brother, Robert Victor Azango, Jr. A special mention must be made to two wonderful souls who brighten my life always: Azama Madasi Momolu and Victor Dumu.

Much appreciation to Various & Gould for allowing us to use their artwork [Wanted Witches – Witches Wanted (Mae Azango), Berlin 2014] for the cover photo. Photo credits the Committee to Project Journalists, CPJ, of New York.

Thank you FORTE Publishing and the entire Monrovia READS Team for making my life richer.

AUTHOR'S NOTE

VOICE OF THE TRUMPETESS, is a reflection on parts of my life. However, many parts of this story are relatable for my readers: the fear during the war years, the hunger, the deaths, the trauma, self-exile, and loss.

The events here are best dealt with as and when they present themselves. We wanted to accomplish a few things with this publication. People often ask me, "Why do you write so passionately about these issues?" My hope is that they will understand by the time they are done reading these pages.

I can identify with most of the situations I am passionate about. My advocacy comes from the past. My experiences make it possible to sympathize and even empathize with most of those whose stories I tell. I lived through abuse: physical, psychological and even sexual. I know how it feels to feel powerless and give up, as happens during rape. I know what it feels like to justify an abusive partner's behavior and even blame oneself for it. I lived through the fear of the next punch, kick, slap or knock by an unknown object.

Importantly, I want anyone going through these things to know that they, too---yes, I mean you---can beat it. You have the power to change your life regardless of those doubts and 'situations' that hinder. I make no illusion that the choices to get away from all of that are easy. They are never easy, but they are worth it. Today, I am free. I am also happy because of the decision to walk away. Abuse in any form is never allowable or justifiable. A life free of it is worth more than everything you left behind, especially the abuser.

.

PROLOGUE

I lay on the cold muddy floor. My stomach is churning, my world spinning, pain shooting through my entire body. I could focus on nothing. I just wanted it to stop.

"Confess!"

"Please stop!" I wanted to scream but could not even do so because my voice was all gone from hours of shouting and wailing.

"Child, I say you mon confess. Dah who you do it with?"

"Nobody," I whispered.

"Dah lie! You belleh tork ehn!"

"I nah lying," I mouthed.

"If you nah stop lying, de baby may live but you wey die! The Spirits will na leh you to live." She continues beating on me as she talks. She has this bamboo rattan, a thin one that leaves red bruises on the skin. I don't even feel the lashes anymore. I'm in more pain than that.

An older man hovers by, chanting. He must be the priest or an intercessor. The shabby room is adorned with bones from dead chickens, birds and other small animals. The hanging baskets each hold some unknown substance. They are all portals for the spirit realms. As he increases his chants, she goes crazy lashing and screaming.

We are at a traditional midwife's residence. I had just delivered my first child. I was still in pain, and for some reason, my placenta refused to come out.

As per tradition, I must have slept with another man, hence the complication. The remedy was a good old-fashioned confession and, voila, delivery will go smoothly.

But I was never unfaithful during my pregnancy. I had no secret lover whose identity I was hiding. I was ignorant to the amount of danger I faced, but I was also determined to keep my dignity.

Regardless of my truth, they were now forcing a confession out of an otherwise 'stubborn' me. I had but one concern: how to stop the pain, now.

All this is happening at lightning speed now. The

baby had come, but my placenta has burst and remains inside of me. The midwife goes crazier than usual, fearing she might lose me. The pain is unbearable. I just wish it to stop.

"Confess nah lay geh, you and yor char way die oh."

"Awww! Oooooh!" I moan.

"Ehn, you sleep with different man?"

"Uhm." I vigorously nodded.

"Ehn hnn, I knew it." she exclaimed. "Weh his name? Call it, say lay name so we mon takor dis baby."

By now, I'm covered in mud and a warm pool of my blood. My life is leaving my body, I can hardly move. I just want this pain to stop. I'd do anything to stop it. "Yes, yes."

"Dah ..." the name drowns out as I begin to feel faint. I am nodding to anything at this point. He chants more; she is also working faster. I am drifting even faster.

"Thank Gor." She utters.

Out of the corner of my eye, I see him bringing a concoction. She takes it, shakes the bottle. Sits on the floor, where I'm reeling slowly. She nestles my head, opens my mouth. Blood is shooting down my thighs. I am bleeding a river. I'm beyond weak.

She pours down my mouth a top full of some bitter portion. I swallow several gulps. I am thirsty for anything now. I don't care. I swallow another, but I cough and spit it out. She claps me down tighter. He steps in to hold me in place as she pours down my throat a top-full of kerosene.

The powerful mixture hits me hard. The room spins, my head pounds, my throat explodes. The room gets darker than usual, everything is dark. I'm in a vortex. I breathed my last breath and blacked out.

VOICE OF THE TRUMPETESS

MAE AZANGO

1

SHATTERED REALITY

Edges Ruffled

My life as a child was not pleasant. Period. Yes, this is a bold claim. I say it not in retrospect alone but because even as a child, I knew unpleasantness. I lived it, breathed it and feared it. Sadly, I think I even came to accept it. It was so regular I believed it was a part of every child's life. Now, with the knowledge I have, I still cringe a bit.

Where I come from, we call it discipline, a stern one. In other parts of the world, they call it physical and psychological abuse. The truth is, growing up was as difficult as it was pleasing.

I was adopted, not with the fanfare of the Qui people. It was a simple transfer of child to family. Obviously, after some previous discussion, my Grandmother, Sarah Carter, who was an aunt of Mrs. Bertha Baker Azango, upped me and dropped me off at the Azango's residence. This was in the 1970's. Things were so different back then.

For some reason, my father, Associate Justice Robert

G.W. Azango, didn't warm to my presence. He missed no chance to let me know his displeasure. He yelled at me and beat me at every given opportunity. It was as if everything I did displeased him. My father wasn't a bad man, but neither was he all good. He was, as is true with any other man, one with flaws. Unfortunately, I bore the brunt of his flawed side and barely experienced the good side.

My mother, Mrs. Bertha Azango, though, was the exact opposite. She loved me beyond anything. She was there for me and gave me everything to make me happy. She did this out of pure love. Not once did I sense she was compensating for my father's treatment of me. I guess this further irritated my father, who showed it in every way possible.

He was a complex man. He showed love at times to the other children. I know firsthand of his generosity. However, just as it is unfair to judge a person by one negative trait, it is equally unfair to do so with a positive one. The sad reality is that we are often fond of making judgments.

Therefore, I lived and quickly found ways to accept those who loved me at home: that included most of the other members of our family.

I recall how my father stiffly opposed the decision by Mommy to attach Azango to my name. He said I should not use his name in school. By that time, he considered me an impostor in his family.

However, my mother always deflected his negativity with a joke. She'd say, "Robert, leave the child alone. Is my name not Bertha Baker Azango? Therefore, Mae is using my share of the Azango name and not yours. Did I not inherit the name when we married?" No matter how he fumed, she tactfully navigated around his anger. Oh, and she was a master at skirting trouble. Thus, I carried the name Mae Azango, and still do.

Yet, as mentioned, my father was complex. I have some fond memories of him. I recall that we used to have Sunday morning prayers and the bigger children would recite the collect each Sunday, whilst the other smaller kids and I would recite Bible verses.

However, one particular Sunday morning, the older children could not recite the collect; they were missing it like nobody's business, and the Oldman was furious. Without being told, I recited it for them. My father could not conceal how impressed he was because he could not understand how I a little girl, could recite their prayers when I could not read the collect much less understand it. The truth is, I had memorized it as the older ones were reading aloud. He stopped them from eating that day as punishment.

He could be generous as well. I'll never forget that he loved dry rice with bitter balls (garden eggs), okra, and pepper. He liked it mixed with red palm oil. Whenever he came home late, he would call me to cook his *pouwon*, as he used to call it, and when I did, he would share it with everyone. All the kids would be happy because our stomachs were stuffed for the night.

Other times, he could be annoying as hell. He had a way of spoiling our meals. He often came home at lunch and ate all his food. But when Mommy came, she was never able to finish all of hers. Everyone kept their hopes up that she'd call us and give the *tip plate* away. We'd then get to share it.

Sometimes, he would ambush her. He did it one of two ways: cunningly or brutishly. When Mommy arrived, he'd wait for her to be at the table and then he'd go sit with her or sit nearby and start up a lecture.

"Bertha, how was your day?"

"It was fine, you?"

"Well, so-so."

"How are the children?   Is everyone behaving?"

"Behaving? Do they know what that means?

"What is it?"

"You know your children...."

And then he would proceed to narrate our 'evil' deeds, after which she'd cut him short with something like: "Was work too tense or something? Or just manageable?"

"Oh it was manageable. No major worries. You?"

"Nothing more than the usual."

At other times, he'd get straight into a topic of interest to her. They'd talk forever. She'd eventually forget the food whilst he took up his seat and commenced bussing that chew.

If he had to be brutish, he'd wait for her to call one of the boys to come clear the table. Just as the person was taking the plates away, he'd yell, "Moses" or whoever it was: "Nobody should eat Bertha's balance rice. Keep it for me."

The often-grumbling person had no choice but to obey.

A few times, we'd pretend not to hear him, but we soon learned that trick didn't go unpunished. It came at the expense of one's hide. Whenever he was ready, he'd call out, "Bring me Bertha's balance food." And just like that, our hopes died. Everyone hated it when he got away with that.

Lust Unleashed

Ideally, during pubescence, a girl's best friend and protector should be selected from among a small pool: her mother, aunts or big sisters. Mine was my big sister, Lovette. Even with that connection, none of us were prepared for the bomb that ensued.

In 1985, just after my pre-teen years, life hurled its most challenging punch: sexual abuse. A close male figure in my family molested me. My experience was not different from most other little girls who are molested in their homes by family members and relatives. Initially, I was cajoled, and then threatened when my perpetrator was not fully convinced I would remain silent about the abuse.

May 10, 1985 is a memorable day in my life for two reasons: it is my sister and best friend's natal day. Secondly, it was the day life revealed to me how, even when you think things could not get any worse, they actually can. The day was wet. Mommy headed a group advocating for women's rights called Woman Development Association of Liberia,

WoDAL, and they were having a walk to raise money for the organization. At that time, a sponsorship citation had to be given to any male relative who oversaw us at home whenever our parents had engagements requiring them to be out most of the day. Mommy left it for the uncle who would watch us.

Sometime during the course of the day, Lovette went out with her friend. For most of the day, they stayed out. I ended up doing most of the chores and having a relaxed day.

The rain continued. The wind howled and there were bursts of thunder and lightening. By late evening, my parents, the children and the rest of the family had supper and retired. Everyone went to his or her rooms. Not too long after we supped, my uncle came home after briefly stepping out. I went off to get him something to eat. As I set the table, the power went out, so I lit candles and waited on him. I then gave him the citation Mommy had left for him.

"Child, you know my eyes are bad. Read that note for me."

****

Innocence Shattered

The dining room was mostly dark as night when I began reading. A few lines into the note, the sound of his utensils clinking against the plate stopped. I passed this off, innocently assuming he'd stopped to listen. As I strained to see the words under the flickering candle, I felt a presence, immediately followed by firm hands gripping my just-forming breasts.

Nothing in my life had prepared me for this, especially not here where I felt safe. My initial reaction was a protective one; I pulled back only to hit into the solid oak utensil cabinet. It didn't budge an inch. Then he advanced a few paces, pinning me with a powerful grip from one hand. I struggled to breathe and I remained still. No fear. No anger. No resentment--- just nothing. It was as if I'd hibernated. In hindsight, I think, my mind locked itself up to guard against the trauma it was experiencing.

In those brief moments, my life didn't flash in front of me. It just stopped. I seemed incapable of functioning. Then, nearly as abruptly as it had locked down, my mind snapped.

I felt a cold breeze on my raw skin and then the touch of strong fingers handling my tender breasts. Nothing about the touch was gentle.

It was raw, harsh and prickly. I realized my clothes had been removed. Most of my blouse was loosened, my buttons ripped off. My bra hung loose under both armpits, swinging along with the wind. The part of the blouse that was intact, stayed stuck around my neck, under his hand that squeezed me and pinned me against the cabinet. Strangely, it was the only thing of comfort during the neck pain---the soft cotton under his hand.

Somewhere in all this, I finally found my voice. My attempts at screams were muffled somewhere among the thunder, the banging of cupboards and windows against their frames, and the drum of raindrops on the roof of the house. With all that noise, my voice didn't amount to much.

He continued to rub me in the most uncomfortable ways. His manhood was now firmly lodged in my tiny fingers with his large hand cupping mine as he stroked himself. Moans and other beastly sounds emanated from him. In the process, I doubt he even remembered that his hand was pressed against my neck.

My frantic struggle for air was lost to him. His eyes burned with a raw, animalistic fire. He was tearing away at anything that hindered him from getting his wish. He'd transformed into a monster I'd never seen but would become familiar with in the near future.

Just as my fight left me and I resolved to the idea that I would not live, the doorbell rang. The loud triple bell sound reverberated through the house but with a much more muffled sound than usual. Whoever was at the door realized that no one would hear them at this time, so they pushed open the door.

Literally, the bells saved me. The gnawish dragging of the heavy oak door against the floor created a louder sound than the bell did. This forced him out of his monstrous rage. His eyes remained fiery as he averted his frenzy towards restoring his garments to their normal state.

As he struggled to get dressed, he offered: "I will give you money, plenty money if you don't tell anyone about this."

By now, an anger rose in me. I was shaking violently. I wanted to scream back at him, "I don't care about your money!" I knew it wouldn't be long now; help was here. The house was big, but with the screen door opened, it wouldn't take long for the person to reach someone in the house.

He raised his head, probably seeing me for the first time in all this. He paused, shook himself and said: "Ehn you want money? Don't worry. I will give you plenty but you can't talk; not to anybody, especially your sister and your parents. Don't tell anybody, okay? I'll leave the door open. You should come inside when they are gone. Your money will be waiting for you, plenty too. Just come, okay?"

I still said nothing. I remained quiet but shook more violently. This time just staring, wanting to choke him as he had done me. I had a resolve not to end this here, on this note. I would not let him narrate this part of my story.

Of course, I didn't know it in these terms then. What I knew right from that moment was that he would not stop.

He had set his eyes on me and I no longer had the luxury of being considered a human being, much less a little girl. I was now a consumable object. By dehumanizing me, he'd rationalized his actions as justifiable, even doable. It was now up to me to stop it or be consumed by it.

This was a harsh reality for a child in her early teens to handle. In fact, there was no handling this. I knew not what to do nor how to do what needed to be done. I knew it had to stop but---nothing more.

He paused briefly, stared at me, and pushed me against the desk, knocking the air out of me and temporarily slowing my shaking body. "If you open your mouth to anyone, you will be in serious trouble. I'll deal with you when your people go out. You'll be dead! In fact nobody will believe you since I will say that you lied."

Clearly sensing my resolve, he now tried to silence me with fear. "You hear me!" he yelled. Just like that, he rushed off into his room. I dragged myself to open the door.

On the other side of it was Lovette. Her boyfriend had brought her home right on time. She was wet from the rain. One look at me forced her to stop and ask: "Mae, what's wrong with you?"

His parting act had succeeded in scaring me. I resumed my uncontrollable shaking. I guess Lovette, being just in from the rain, figured if there was to be any shaking, it should be from her. "Nothing!" I tried to mouth---but not a sound came from between my lips.

I was unable to process the shock that a man I grew to love and respect almost all my life wanted to rape me. I could not understand why it was happening to me. My mind raced with questions: "Had I done something to provoke him? What drove him to the thought?" I was conscious of my body's changes. Mommy had given me the 'talk' in part. Still....

It just didn't feel right in my little head. I didn't know what 'it' was, but I knew it was inappropriate to do it now, more so with a relation.

I now had another problem. Lovette wanted to know. I had no answers for her, sadly. I had none for me. She had put on that I-am-not-taking-no-for-an-answer face. Whenever she wore it, she got her way. I toyed with the idea of the truth! However, that was scary, at least after the threats from my uncle a few moments earlier. A lie seemed appropriate. I didn't know then that life presents these situations where one would feel an urge to willfully lie. Here I was desperately searching for a lie to give my best friend and sister, even when I knew she'd see right through it. Yet, it seemed like the best idea at the time. I wasn't even considering the morality dimensions. I had to deflect her questions any way possible, if I wanted to live.

But after a while, no longer capable of resisting the persistently harassing Lovette, I finally summoned the courage to tell her what had happened. By now, we had gone to her room where I had earlier planned to deliver her birthday present.

"What?" She pulled back to stare me down. "You're joking with me, right?" Everything about my appearance told her otherwise.

I nodded, whispering a soft, "True."

She sat me down and talked me through it. I don't recall how much detail I retold.

"You know what, don't say anything just yet. Let me handle this, okay? You must promise me to keep quiet about it. Do not tell anyone. You can't go running that loud mouth of yours with this kind of thing. You hear me?"

"Yes."

"I am not joking. Let me see what to do about this. Until then, stay away from him."

"Okay. But why would he do that?"

"I find it hard to comprehend. Maybe he was on one of his drunken sprees. You know how it is when he drinks, right? The truth is I still can't believe all this, not from him."

Thus, we ended our conversation. We decided to see what would happen the next day. If he was drunk, he'd have no recollection of his actions; if not, he might attempt again.

To my utmost surprise, the next morning, a Saturday, when my parents and sister went for a walk, my attacker rang the doorbell and my cousin went to answer. He told my cousin to call me. When I went to him, he asked: "Why did you not come to my room after I left the door open for you? Anyway, it is not too late. Come, let's go now."

"I am cooking," was all I could manage. I distinctly recall the sinking feeling as my heart felt as if it had dropped in the pit of my belly. I think this was my first time ever feeling disgust, pit-wrenching disgust. It didn't feel as much hateful as one would think. It felt depressing, and troubling, but more on the low end of the way one feels when news of a death is broken. He was indeed dead to me. Whatever anger I may have felt previously paled in comparison to the heavy emptiness I now felt.

Now I think I know how it is possible for one to remove all humanness from a person and treat them as trash. I didn't feel anything for him. I only felt something from within me, and those thoughts were not nice. They were not directed at a human being it seemed; at least not right then. I wanted to lash out at an object, for in those moments, I saw him as nothing more than an object.

It took a while after walking away for me to feel anger. I was livid, but not sure at what exactly. Him, his actions, words, the dehumanizing look on his face, his lust for my young forming body. I did not know which; perhaps a bit of all.

I returned to the kitchen and told his nephew what his uncle had said, and asked if I should report it to my parents. Instead, he told me not to say a word before I break up his uncle's marriage.

I did not go to his room after I got through cooking, but waited for my sister to come. Immediately, as she walked through the door that evening, I told her: "He tried again."

"Really?" Then she said: "So he knew exactly what he was doing last night and he was pretending to be drunk. I will have to deal with this, I just need small time. I want to do something first. Still, say nothing and stay away from him. If we are not careful, it could turn around on you."

On the following Monday morning, she went to our Aunt Grace Morris' house to ask her for advice.

"My child, this is shocking!"

"I know, Teta Grace."

"And how long ago you say this happened? You mean you did not tell anybody about it? Why are you just telling me?" She fired away question after question, not waiting for a response. It was not hard to see that she was more angry than shocked. For a brief moment, I almost felt she was allowing her anger to have the better of her. She began to sound as if we'd done her the worse by not telling her earlier. I later understood her fears, as well as why she reacted the way she did.

"You better go tell your folks."

"Yes, Teta Grace."

"Do you hear me?"

"Yes I do." Lovette muttered.

"Tell Bertha before I reach that house and do it for you. He could overpower this lil'o char one day and rape her. You see how he is much bigger and far stronger. If you delay, that is what might happen."

2

UNMASKING THE DEVIL

The Telling

So we decided to tell Mommy. The next morning, Lovette and I went into her room early. She was a bit concerned to see the two of us barging in that early, more so together. She figured we wanted something, so she ushered us closer. When we were close enough, Lovette said: "Mommy, Mae has something to tell you."

"What? Mae's boyfriend says he doesn't want her?"

No one says anything.

"Mae missed her period? Or Mae is pregnant?"

"Mommy just wait; let Mae tell you herself"

"Okay Mae, what is it you wish to say?"

"Mommy, remember how you gave me a citation the other day for your walk?"

"Yeah,"

"Well, I did as you asked. I went to deliver it after you all had left for work and school. But as I did ...." Then I told her.

"Are you sure about what you are saying?"

"Mommy, I have never talked to you before about such a thing. Why would I lie now? I am sure."

Lovette spoke. "It is true, Mommy. Since Friday, he has attempted twice. Each time he does, Mae comes and reports the incident to me. I told her to stay away from him, hoping he was only drunk the first time, but he did it again. We even went to Teta Grace and told her. She suggested we tell you.

"It is true, Mommy," I chimed in quietly.

The rage in her face could not be hidden. She looked disappointed beyond words. Mommy was always a calm person. Her continence showed a furious woman I had never before seen--- nor would I ever see her this way until her death.

"When did this happen, you say? And you are sure that is all that happened?"

"Yes, mom"

"Nothing more? He only had you fondle him,"

"Yes, mom."

"And then he touched you and did nothing more?"

"Yes mom, I swear."

"You told your sister, and she said you should wait?

"Yes, Mommy."

"Okay, you did well. Just wait here. I will be back."

I stood transfixed. My fear had left me. A small part of me feared that she would not believe me. I admit that I had no reason for this, but I guess the initial disbelief expressed by the first people I told led me to expect the same from Mommy. I had never before felt safer nor respected Mommy more than I did at that point. She looked at me with nothing but anguish in her eyes, beneath which was a love that she rarely displayed this overtly. Don't get me wrong. I knew Mommy loved me, but the culture of our times discouraged overt display of such affection unless it was necessary. Even at that, the conditions of necessity were fluid and mostly determined only by the parent or adult. In a few moments, Mommy showered me with more affection than I'd probably received in a lifetime before then.

Strange how, amidst all this, I could zero in on her reaction and not the gravity of the situation. I guess I'd been dealing with that for some time now, but this was new or just unexpected; I could not miss it.

The Confronting

Mommy left us girls in the room and went to confront the culprit. It took us a while to realize that, but when we did, Lovette went to eavesdrop. In our times, children didn't listen in on adult conversations. It was considered rude. Lovette was taking a huge risk here, but one we believed was worth it.

"…. It is a bloody lie!"

"Really?"

"Really? How would you even believe that little lying girl over me?"

"I know my daughter; she will not just lie on you."

"How can you people? I mean, this is me you are talking about, not some stranger."

"Which is precisely why we are doing this! If it were anyone else, it would be a different story."

"I did no such thing."

"So why would she lie on you?"

"I don't know! You ask her. Maybe she hates me. Or she'd rather see me in trouble. I have no idea."

"You can't say that and expect me to believe it."

"So you take that pissy liar's words over mine?"

"You leave me with no choice. Mae may lie like any other child, but on this, I tend to believe her. She has nothing to gain. Have you seen her lately? Noticed anything new about her? Strange, in fact?"

"I am not even paying attention to her!"

"Well, this is what she has said. Is this all you can say?"

"I swear that girl is evil. She hates me. Why else would she lie on me this way?"

"I don't believe she is lying."

"She is! In fact, don't ever bring her here again. I don't want to ever see her. If you insist, then she should have nothing to do with me. Nor should she touch anything of mine."

"Oh, I don't intend to ever leave you alone with her. Not ever!"

"Good. Settled then!"

"No it is not! You should be ashamed of yourself. How low must one sink to even entertain such an idea? Be warned, you have not heard the end of this matter."

"Just make sure you keep her away from this house and from me specifically."

"Oh you need not bother with that; you will never be trusted with her again!"

"Better!"

"Yes, better!"

"Who the hell is Mae that she would try to ruin my reputation?"

"She is my daughter...."

Lovette rushed into the room, "Mae, I think we better leave this house. We must go home. I don't think we are safe here any longer! Mommy thinks that much. I feel the same!"

****

The Healing

My family's support and reaction played a major role in my healing. I cannot overstress this point. Families need to respond with clear messages and unwavering support in these situations. It is easy for victims to feel alone, rejected.

It is even harder to shake off the notion that "I must have done something to deserve this. Perhaps I provoked this reaction." Even though I knew I did no such thing, I still had moments when I felt as though I may just have triggered it.

I survived this mostly because my family stood by me and repeatedly reminded me that this was not my fault. The more I heard this, the more I believed it. It did not matter what I thought I knew before. It mattered though, that others who I love could validate what I knew to be true.

One who has never been in a situation like that would hardly understand how something as little as that is a lifesaver. The constant reminders that I was okay and in no way responsible for anything that happened lifted my trust in humans again. For many days after the incidents, I felt foreign, alone, discouraged. I graduated from fear, to anger, and then I got livid. Eventually, I hated. I hated my culprit. I hated this confused state. I simply hated.

I could deal with it, however, because of the strong support my family lent me. My folks, mostly Mommy, drew closer to me than usual. We developed a special relationship. She used the opportunity to teach me how to cook, bake, and be a woman. But more importantly, she instilled in me a fight for justice. I see my advocacy as an extension of the cause she and a few women of their times began.

She often said, "Mae, in our times, women are heard less and seen more." However, all the while she was leading a fight for women's suffrage. At a time when women were relegated to the background, she educated herself, earning a doctorate. Teta Grace, well let's wait to see if she pops up again somewhere in these pages.

My sister remained by my side even up to this day; she is my most valued confidant. My brother Robert Jr. (commonly known as Victor) refused to speak to the culprit ever. He effectively cut ties for life.

Based on the strong support of my family, that is, the small circle who knew about the incidents, I can clearly state I was luckier than most others who fall victim.

The next logical question I guess you are all asking is why am I not shaming and naming here? It was no easy choice to even dig deep into my suppressed memories and write about this incident. Nevertheless, for some time now, I have not been in doubt about telling others about this part of my life. I am convinced that some could benefit from it.

Equally, I see no gain in naming, primarily because the culprit is dead. No, I am not afraid to speak ill of the dead, if they did do something evil. My upbringing and my own discipline demand more of me.

I could say in earnest I watched that man wither away and saw parts of him die slowly, as his family members and loved ones cut him off forever. I saw a once proud man, whose ego was larger than the moon, go out of his way to reconcile. I saw a man humbled by circumstances and, in his own way, truly repentant. Do I pity him? No! I don't. Do I empathize? How can I? Yet, I am human enough to know when to let go. My family took enough steps, hence I could let go.

I refused to give any part of me to that hate or non-forgiveness. I refused to carry him around long before he reached the point of repentance. I just could not afford him any more than what he took. He may not have penetrated me, but I did not feel any less raped. Any victim will tell you that penetration is only the physical pain. The psychological and emotional trauma I felt no less. My case is not any better on that account.

I shuddered; I was scared and had nightmares for a time after the incidents. I withdrew. I felt vulnerable. As far as my body was concerned, I was as good as raped, mentally and emotionally.

3

SHENANIGANS

Caught in the Act

You know how it is that children grow up with one bad habit or another? Let us just say I had one too many. If there was one thing I knew I excelled in at home, when discussing our shenanigans, it was being a fast finger. I took sweets and was caught in the cookie jars way more than I care to admit. I could not resist the urge to pick through food for meat or fish.

Ironically, today many people bring their valuables and cash to me for safe-keeping. What they don't know is that I used to be a fast finger.

For some time, people believed that there was a cat in our house. No one had seen it, but we all *knew* it existed because we felt its effects ever so oft.

One day, they'd cooked a favorite local soup of mine. I had my full serving, yet I craved the meat and fish from the others' food. I set an ambush. By late afternoon, it paid off. Everyone was sitting outside in the yard or on the porch 'lecturing'. No one was paying mind to anything or anyone for that matter. It was all about the conversation. Our parents were out; we had the house all to ourselves. What was there not to be happy about?

In the midst of this, I snuck into the kitchen. After inspecting the other bowls, it turned out most of us had eaten all our food. I proceeded to the oven, where we used to keep leftover food that we hadn't eaten and were keeping for later, and the food that had been untouched.

My cousin was the only one who had not touched hers yet. I opened the oven and picked around for the biggest meat. I took a moment to savor the smell and imagine how it would feel on my tongue and between my teeth. Satisfied it had served its purpose, I raised it to my mouth to bite through. Just then, my brother barged in: "Ehn hnn, I got you. So it is you who have been stealing people's meat in the house?"

The saliva that comes just before a bite turned sour in my mouth. It was just at the base of my tongue but not yet in my throat. This would eventually turn into bile. My fingers froze, my hand shook, my heart raced and my mind exploded. I could form no words. I was in a most awkward situation and, for once, I could utter not a word.

"Now, you just walk outside with the meat in your hand."

I wished the ground to split but no such thing happened.

"Let's go!" He barked.

Thus, we went outside. He paraded me in the yard. The boys soon started chanting, "Meat rogue! Meat rogue!"

He asked them to stop, only to tell them: "As you all can see, this is the cat that has been eating all the meat from our food."

"This is no small cat, oh." Someone chimed in.

They all burst out laughing and continued their variants of the meat rogue song. Of course, you can guess how this ended--- with a good flogging that left my buttocks bruised. Through it all, I said nothing. I guess because I was guilty, it felt justified. But it was more than that. The thing is, in our society then, nothing was wrong with strict discipline. I could have reported them to my parents but I'd have most likely suffered another round of beating or some other form of punishment. What I do know is that I never did that again. That day, the cat lost its ninth life and died. The focus was on correcting a wrong and using punishment as a deterrent.

No one saw this as abuse. No one saw those boys as bullying. This kind of thing happened and one found a way to deal. It was that simple. The 'unspared rod' or fear of it drove parents and society into imposing Puritan-like afflictions on their wards. No one wanted an unspared-rod-like, unruly child. There were few enabling conditions in society for 'victims' to address their 'abuses'. If one was wrong, one got punished. It was as simple as ABC. One did not have to think it over. Things were simpler then; solutions were fitted to the environment.

I am not dabbling into the discipline/abuse debate. However, I will say this: we use hindsight and our current disposition to judge the past. That alone ensures that we will find serious problems with the past. This trend may work for us now, but also ensures that those coming after us will employ similar methods when speaking to our morality and psychosocial processes.

Little Miss Fast

Apart from stealing meat from in my siblings' food, I was also a fast mouth. They called me a parrot, because not only did I say things I had no business saying or I always reported what I said, but because I was fond of doing things spontaneously---most of which I had no business doing.

There was one time when my brother got so angry with me. Robert Junior played high school basketball. He often stayed after school for practice. That day, his girlfriend and her friends came by the house.

"Hello, Mae."

"Hello, my brother sweetheart." She smiled.

"Is Robert here?"

"No, he is not."

"Hmmm."

"What happened?"

"Uh... nothing much. We are just hungry from all that walking."

"Oh, sorry oh, but no food here. I ate all of mine and so has everyone else. Only Robert still has food here."

"Oh, really? Okay, where is his food? Bring it, I will tell him I ate it. Go bring it quick, before I faint."

Just like that, I had landed myself into trouble. The funny thing is, I expected Robert to be angry about this---but not as angry as he was when he found out.

"You what?" he barked.

"I gave the food to her."

"Who told you to do that?"

"She said she was hungry bad way."

"So?"

"No, but she wor with her friend dem."

"Dah your chew before you gave it out? Dah me supposed to feed them?"

I have no response for this so I fidget.

"How did she even know where my food was? Answer me? She jeh asked you and it flew to her?"

"No, I went for it and they ate."

"You gave her ALL my food? Uh, hmmmn. See how stupid you can act? You nah even takor sommor ley whacking seh. You jeh gay ley whole bowl. Now, I hungry lek dat en nothing here. Bor I way flog you today, you way nah makor yorseh."

"Bor I nah do nothing bad. Ehn dah yor gehfriend?" I protested.

"I way beat you bahr way today."

Truthfully, I wasn't innocent here. That dude flogged me so often, I wanted to pay him back anyway I could. The best way I figured to get back for his whacking, since he loved food business more than anything else under this sun, was to give his away. Unfortunately, it just backfired on me.

"Hug the pole, and two lashes for one when you remove your hands."

Thus, I got another round of beating. Such was common in our times. It is not as if I was the easiest person to live with. I could be bullheaded.

However, I wasn't always guilty. There was one time I was punished that etched itself in my mind.

Beaten for my brother's crime

I often slept with Mommy, who was always afraid after she watched horror movies. In fact, as the youngest child, I could sleep anywhere I wanted, mostly. Other times, when my Mom locked her door early, I slept with my big sisters. Usually my mother used me as an alarm clock. On school days, she'd send me to wake up the big children, so that they could prepare breakfast and do their housework before leaving for school. Victor was not fond of this, none of them were, but he was the cunning one, always finding ways around it.

The previous night, when I found my mom's door locked, I went to my sisters' room. But they had positioned themselves in a way that I could not even find a comfortable space to squeeze myself into. I went to Victor's room to ask if I could sleep with him, since my sisters had no space for me. He agreed, and I hopped in his bed and slept.

The next morning, it was raining heavily. It was the kind of morning when people really enjoy their sleep. Along comes Mommy, waking people up. She knocked at my brother's door first, and then the bigger girls' door. When they would not wake up, she got angry and went for her cane to whip them.

When she returned, the first door she pushed open was my brother's. But he heard her when she said she was coming back to whip them, so he covered me nicely under the covers and hid in the closet. She reached the bed and started whipping me with her full might, all the while thinking it was Victor. I jumped up yelling. Mommy stopped. Her face told it all. Apparently, Mommy had sprung a trap for him this time, only to catch the wrong child. I told you he was tricky whilst growing up.

He ran out of the closet laughing. It was so funny that my mom started laughing whilst petting me. "Never mind, my dear, I did not know it was you, baby. I thought it was Victor, but I will deal with him." Mistake or not, her lashes were solid; they hurt so bad that I felt it in my soul. That lesson was enough for me not to ever make such a mistake like that again.

Brewed in the Past

Remember how I said that from as far back as I can recall, my mouth has landed me in a few tight spots? Only a few, I kid you not. I often got flogged by my siblings not because I lied, stole a cube of sugar or two to secretly lick, or took some cookies without asking. Oh, all these I did and then some.

I suspect they used these acts as excuses to cover the fact that I was often flogged because I was a pepper bird. They didn't hesitate to remind me during my discipline that my mouth ran like a bird.

One such birdy instance happened on a Sunday. We children prepared and left for church service, but never made it to the church. This meant that our offerings didn't make it to the collection plate, either.

When we returned home that evening, Mommy asked: "Mae, what's new?"

Without prompting, I replied: "Mommy, we did not go to Sunday school today. We went to Careysburg and used the offering money to buy palm wine."

"Really?" she inquired.

"Yes Mommy, that's what we did."

"So how did you go there?"

"We used your car. It was Boy Jessie who drove us around." When Mommy knew it was her car, she was angry. To exact her revenge, she summoned all the bigger children and said: "Mae tells me that you all went to Careysburg for palm wine instead of going to church. What do you have to say?" That was how Mommy was: to-the-point. She ended up punishing them by making them weed a sizable portion of grass in the yard. Of course, my behind suffered the next day after she left for work.

4

1990

July 13 [Morning hours]

Introduction

Friday the 13th: I remember while I served breakfast, I overheard Mommy tell Daddy in a low tone: "Robert, do you know today is Friday the 13th? This is a bad day, possibly even the death of many people."

My father dismissed her by saying; "Ohooo Bertha, that is a superstitious belief. Do not tell me you also believe that this day is bad."

It had been raining the whole week---as it does only in the midst of the Liberian rainy season. Dark clouds choked the sky, draining themselves of their contents. Just when the rain eased up to a light drizzle, we heard strange dialects from near the back of our fence. They grew louder. Later, we found out that they were speaking Gio. Somehow, these people must have entered our yard in order for them to sound this close.

Just then, they barged into our compound, "Weh le dam gorwormen people dah living here? Yor bring yor a##es orside before I break ley door!" one shouted.

"If yor nah come before I say fah, monkeys wey die here oh." Another said.

We trembled in our beds awaiting something, anything.

"Bor weh yor standing here for? Yor go insah and drag de dam gorwormen connaper orsah here."

"Open ley door and come orsah!"

The next instant, they made their way into our home.

The people speaking looked raw and fearful. They had chalk marks on parts of their bodies as well as a mixture of wigs, weave-ons, masks, caps and hats. Some were half-naked. Others wore women's clothes and makeup, whilst others could pass as any regular person.

They lined us up single file and out into the yard. To our surprise, some of our neighbors were with them. They had accompanied the group to our house because my father was a government official and he was living there. Little did we know that an altercation some time past would lead to this.

During one holiday season, I can't recall which, people had brought in some Gio traditional stilt dancers to perform, which was disturbing others in the neighborhood. The neighbors reported the Gio dancers to Daddy. Being an officer of the court, my father informed them that they could not have the performance---especially not an all-night affair---without duly informing the authorities, who would have granted them a permit.

Since they did not have a permit, and their neighbors were complaining, he had no choice but to have the authorities shut it down. The Gio held that grudge. Now, it seemed, they had a chance for revenge. When they left, the rebels took away our parents. That was our first brush with the freedom fighters.

Some Action

We'd all lost track of time. These rebels had been at it for what seemed like hours. In truth, it was about an hour.

The psychological abuse, the threats, and the mild physical abuse: we could never have been prepared for these things. We just endured whatever they threw at us. When they were satisfied they'd gathered enough loot, they dragged Mommy and Daddy out of the yard.

"Bor chief, weh we mon do way ley children dem?"

"Weh you asking me for? You nah know wetting to do? Dis man dah dead meat already. We jeh taking him to the G-2 office on the road." They were speaking of our lives as if we were not there. It was clear we had no part in this decision. Just up by Joe Bar was a small G-2 checkpoint created by the fighters.

As they left, the few rebels left behind had a plan of their own. They began speaking their dialect again. It soon turned into an argument. "So, dah we ley one mon nah enjoy too ehn?" One ventured.

"Bor lah order de chief gay."

"What order ehn?"

"He say we mon fini ley people."

"Lah wha he say?" the first one asked another rebel, who had not spoken a word through all this. His friend nodded. "I nah hear him say dah oh. He only ass if we nah know wetting to do to ley people dem."

"My mehn, we mon nah waste our time here. Leh take what we can take and go! Don't mind dis foolee man. Anytime we go somewhere, dah only he and hay man dem mon take ley value dem. Me pah, today, I nah leaving out."

"So dah wetting you think we mon do since you know everything?"

"We mon take our own and go. If we dehlay ley people we wey nah geh anything. So leh lee dem and take our own."

Thus, we lived another day, but only after they took what they wanted and warned us not to leave or tell anyone what happened. It was apparent that they would be back. We had no doubt. We had now become pawns in their group politics.

We could not leave without Mommy and Daddy, at least not just yet. We had to discover their fates. That meant someone going after them to the G-2 office. But the last group had just threatened us not to do that. Unsure of what to do, we stayed, and figured we would wait it out. A few hours later, Mommy came back home, but Daddy was left behind at the G-2 office to be investigated further. By 5 p.m.,

Daddy entered the compound. He had been flogged on the head, with gun butts and other objects, for hours. They wanted him to produce the Government of Liberia's money. We found out the hard way that the freedom fighters demanded 'the people's money' from each government employee they caught. It was worse for officials--- and Dad was one big fish.

We attended to his wounds as best as we could, but we were under no illusions that our problems were anywhere near over. No one had ever suggested that this rebel-coming business would result in violence against ordinary people. Now that I reflect, it was quite foolish of many Liberians to think that the rebels would only come and remove President Doe and his kin; that no one else would be caught up in the process. The reality showed differently.

Over the next few days, every other batch of rebels who came to our area entered our compound, because in their search for government employees, our home was always pointed out. We never really knew which of our neighbors sent them our way, but they kept coming. Every time, they had some weird demand or another, and every time they abused us however they wished. Mommy just could not stand it any longer, so she pushed for leaving. Daddy, who got the lion's share of the beatings, was in no position to move. We would have to carry him if we left. Plus, he was afraid to leave, since the rebels kept telling him not to 'flee'. They needed him to go to the Papay, in this case, Charles Taylor. One day in July, Mommy decided she had had enough. She said she had a bad feeling about things and did not wish us staying another day.

35

Road Action

During this time, I was pregnant. In fact, I was about eight months into my pregnancy---another reason Mommy decided not to move earlier. The boys would have had to carry Daddy and me around. This was too much stress.

I remember my fear. I feared my parents would be killed. I feared we all would be killed---but most of all, I feared for my unborn child. I wondered what kind of world he would be born into or if he'd even be born. I could live with having to die. What I could not bear was having my son meet a horrible end.

By now, we had heard stories of how rebels and soldiers were taking babies out of pregnant women's stomach for experiments and for ritualistic purposes.

Some wanted innocent blood for its reputed magical powers, whilst others did it simply because they could. Whichever it was, I was unprepared to be an experiment or have my baby used for some superstitious religious ritual.

Powerless I may have been, prepared to die if it came to that, but determined was I not to allow anything bad to happen to my child. I intended to have that baby before anything happened to me.

5

DANGEROUS TIMES

Spoilt Fruit

Mommy was angry when I got pregnant just before the war, but it turned out to be a blessing in disguise. When the rebels entered the Paynesville-to-GSA general area on July 2, 1990, they did many things: the terrible 'DuPort Road Massacre' foremost amongst them. The checkpoint at that junction had become a death trap. No one passing that route could miss the *mountain of skulls*---fresh and old, it didn't matter. That was a gauge of the scale of killing at that point.

On any given day, the rebels' random searches revealed government employees or some other perceived enemy. There were always enough to pick from and kill. No one ever got used to it.

One day, when we were home, some fighters entered the yard. As they conducted their looting, one spotted me and screamed.

"What happened?" another asked.

"Bad luck!"

"Bad luck? Where?"

"There!" He pointed my way.

I was startled. I didn't know what to make of this reaction. I was seated in the corner, ever-fearful of the fighters.

"Come here!" He ordered, gesturing in my direction. I looked around, despite knowing I was the only one in the corner. I checked around again then he shouted, "Ehn I say you mon bring yor puff up she here?"

"Oh dah ley big belleh you torking aborh?" another asked.

I stood a decent distance away from him, staring skeptically. "Wetting you doing here?"

The question surprised me. "I living here." I offered.

"You living here? How come I nehwor see you before?"

"I living here and I have seen you."

"Oh gbah, lee our big belleh alone mehn. Every day we come here, she lor be here." His friend chimed in, joking.

"No oh my mehn, we nah sorpo to be seeing dis bad luck. Only fresh jue dem we wan. Big belleh dem nah good."

"You pah, you ready again ehn. Leh jeh take our meat we came for and go. Plenty fresh fruits orsah der to eat. Bor nah nah, dah meat we come here for."

"You lucky he torking for you because today pah, yor ownor bisney fini."

I stood transfixed, livid and wishing to reach across and squeeze the tiny frame that dare speak those words, but I knew that would have ended up bad for my family. Instead, I fought to control those hormones raging inside me.

"Ehn you hear me? Ley ness time I come here, I nah wan see you. You mon run anytime you hear say we coming. Noballay coming be seeing bad luck here."

Ripe Fruits

One reality that I fortunately escaped was having to become a rebel wife or girlfriend. The fighters would take any young girl they wished to have and carry her off to their base.

There was this one time we were lined up single file. The commander at this gate sent out his boys to inspect the line for young fresh fruits. Their guns were loaded and cocked; it took only slight pressure on the trigger and that would be the end of the person on other side of the gun.

We were further down the line, closer to the middle. As they came along, they took whatever girl they liked, the younger the better.

"You, move from the line." Parents were powerless to protest. Too much had happened before our eyes. No one here could resist. We were all frightened and broken.

"This one here looking good. Join de ollor people owor der."

"You too." Another was picked.

"My mehn, yor mon take fine fine chic dem oh. Yor know

le CO wey eat hay own fwest before he gay our own dem."

The two people immediately before me were elderly, so the rebels were uninterested. As one came up in front of me, he sneered. "What is dis nonsense?"

I said nothing; my legs were shaking as my entire body trembled. "We looking for juicy fruit then dis rotten one here. You spoil already. No ballay coming be looking at the fruit weh de bweh dem nah ee."

The other one said. "If I count from one to fah and you nah disappear, you wey see whetting I way do to you."

I did not need to be told twice. I ran off the line and headed in the general direction of the nearest clutter of trees. I was just running to get out of a clear line of shot.

Dead Fruits

By this time, the GSA road reeked of death. The air was filled with the fruit of life. More like the fallen fruit: men, women, children, it did not matter. The war had come and it was claiming its toll in humans and kind. It took from everyone. Tribe, social status, education, sex and age did not matter. It demanded its own price and people had to pay.

A friend's father was so unfortunate. He went out to hustle up some food but never returned. The story his family heard was that he encountered rebels, who took him for interrogation.

"You, weh play you going?"

"I am going home. My house is reh around the corner."

"You lying!" one added.

"I nah lying."

"I know all ley people da living here, you nah living here." He tried convincing them but it was not working.

"In faseh, weh kinna werk you doing?

"I am a teacher."

"Chief ley man can lie. He gorwormen official. Dey ley one dem dah wor eating ley people money. So weh play yor hide our money, eh?" the boss asked.

"I am not a government official."

"Da lie, I say. Okay, weh yor ID card eh?" the boss asked.

"I left it home. I did not know I was supposed to travel with it."

"So if you nah gorwormen official why you geh big stomach like this? Ehn dah ley people money yor wor eating fullor yor gut so?" another one asked.

"Oh bossman, I am not a government official. I am just a teacher."

"Okay, you say you living here, come go show us yor house."

"I came to look for food so we can eat. But I live on the other side of the road."

"Oh, so you nah living reh here again?"

"It is nah far from here."

"Where nah, go show us ley place so we mon know you torking ley true."

"It jeh around Rehab."

"Weh play deh cor Rehab? Ehn you say you wor living around here?"

"Chief, ley man lying. Maybe ley man dah AFL. He's on reconnaissance. Dah mission he on."

"I nah no AFL. I am a teacher."

"Oky dah which school you teaching to? Dah church school?"

"No."

"Dah Catholic school?"

"No."

"Da weh kinna school nah?"

"Dah public school."

"Public school?"

"Yes."

"Da weh kinna school dey call public school?" the boss asked one of his men.

"Dah ley school dem own by ley government."

"Ehn I teh you ley man dah gorwormen official? See hay big gut der? Weh kinna teacher fat like dat and having big belly? Only gorwormen people geh big gut. So you wor lying to us?"

"I am not lying. I am just a teacher."

"Fwest, you say you living around here. Then you say dah Rehab you living. You know weh play it eh? Dah far play."

"It is not far." The man interrupted.

"Dah lie, my friend here say ay far. Ay nah even near here. He say ay on ley ollor side of town."

"It is not true. Rehab is just around here, if you bend on the right from this junction, you go down the road small you will reach to Rehab. If you take the short cut behind here, it is even faster."

"Ehn you see chief, ley man know all ley back road dem. Ley man dah enemy connaper. Weh we wasting time with him for? Leh dirty ley man."

Sensing that he was getting nowhere, he just kept quiet. Anyone who'd lived some time with these guys knew that they'd not go through all this trouble just to let you go. They were out for blood and there was no stopping it.

"Okay, if you say you nah gorwormen official and you living reh near here, take us to your house leh see if dah true you torking."

"Okay let's go, I will take you there."

The commander then spoke their dialect and ordered them to get some government money from him and kill his entire family along with him, once they were in possession of the money.

He could understand the language but could not speak it. "Oh chief, why will you do such a thing? I understood the instruction you gave your boys."

"So you my country man? Okay speak it nah."

43

"No, I can't speak it but I understand it."

"Dey man dah AFL, chief. Dey ley one dah learn to understand our dialects so they can trap us and kay us. Dah why he can't speak ay."

Thus, they insisted he take them to his house to prove his innocence. He refused to do that, since he knew his family would meet a similar fate, so they killed him.

6

MORE DANGER

Abduction

One day, our cousins left for the market to get anything available. Whilst there, some of the fighters called: "Ehn dah your living in da big house in de corner? We hear dat your geh one papay there and your can be hiding him in the ceiling. We here sacrificing our lef for yor and yor hiding men dem."

"Yeah oh, dam ungrateful people. Bor the thing dah make me veh is dah ley man dah gorwormen official," his friend jumped in, cutting him short.

"Bor lemme the yor somtin, we coming to da huss tomorrow to check. We way scatta de whole place, if we fahn any man der, we way kay allor yor. We fwehting for yor den yor hiding good good recruit and enemy connapers dem."

Our cousins hurriedly left the market and came home.

They called all the children together and explained. We then decided to go to our aunts and the other elders to explain. We did that and they agreed that we meet with Mommy. I knew that it would break her heart if I was amongst the group that told her, so, I told the other children to go ahead. I had to breastfeed my son; I would join them once I was done. Thus they left.

"Aunty Bertha, hello," one greeted her.

"Hello. How are you? You're okay?"

"Yeah, we are."

"Fine, oh Oldma," another said.

"You wanted to see me? Well, I'm here." Mommy said.

"Yeah, we do. You know that you are our Oldma and we like you but what we are about to say, ay nah easy."

"Okay, you are scaring me now. What is it?" Mommy fired away.

"One of the girls heard the commander's boys saying that they would come from house-to-house searching for men to join the fight. If they find any man in any house, they say they would kill everybody in the house , along with the man they find. ."

"What? Are you sure?" Mommy asked.

"Yes, Oldma, I heard it myself."

"We like you and are grateful for the help you been giving us, but we want to live, too."

"The Oldman nah live his lef, sommon us nah do anything yet. We nah coming to die for hay business."

"I understand. Let me talk to Robert and get back to you."

Mommy considered what the girls had just revealed about the plans of the rebels. In their effort to recruit abled-bodied men and boys, they were doing a house-to-house search. They had by now wised up to the fact that many people had survived by hiding in their ceilings or attics. They intended to search even those inaccessible places. This was troubling, because we too had taken to hiding Daddy in the attic of the house---something necessitated by his latest near-death experience.

~~~

During one of his interrogations, they kept asking Daddy to produce the government's money. After repeatedly telling them he did not have it nor did he know where the money was, he figured a way out.

He said that when the commander went outside, he negotiated with the boys left to guard him. He suggested that they take him home, where he could give them some money. The one in charge saw a rare opportunity. He dispatched Daddy under the guard of two men. As they left, he instructed them in their local dialect to kill him once they received the money. He said they should do so along the way back, and dispose of the body in the swampy area. That way, no one would find him--- not even the boss. It was a simple plan that would screw the commander out of his loot. I guess he believed he was about to score a huge windfall, considering Daddy was a Supreme Court justice. He figured

Daddy had to have had tons of cash lying around somewhere, or at least easy access to plenty government funds. What he did not know was that Daddy had spent some time in Nimba and understood their language.

He said nothing until they reached the house. The rebels explained to Mommy what their mission was. She gave them the last $1,500 we had on and they set off to go.

"Papay, come let's go see our boss nah?"

"My children, I am tired. Yor please lemme rest smor. Yor know I nah going anywhere. Just hurry and take the money to your boss before he gets vex. After I rest, your can come back for me."

"Bor Papay, ay too dark, we can't see, why don't you carry us half way so we can use yor flashlight?"

"Yor wan see, take de light, I will collect it tomorrow." Daddy offered.

To our surprise, they left with the money. That is why we began hiding Daddy in the attic of the house.

When they left, he explained that the commander had instructed them to kill him after taking the money. They were supposed to do it on their way back, because their boss did not want them to kill Daddy in front of his wife and the children.

Whenever a new group of rebels came by to collect our goats, sheep, pigs or other animals, they'd ask after him. We'd say he wasn't there, and that the previous commander had taken him away. We always lied that we did not know where he was.

The rebels usually seemed more interested in getting their hands on the animals than on Daddy. When there were no more farm animals, they took the dogs; and when those got finished, they got irritated and looked for a reason to get rid of us. It became clear that we had served our usefulness and were thus expendable.

After the girls revealed the rebels' plan, Mommy went to consult with Daddy. This was a test of our resolve. Daddy was still recovering from the injuries. The attic was not exactly the best place to do that, but at least he was alive. But once we got this news, we had to do what we had been avoiding from the onset of this drama. No one wanted to say it, but Daddy had to go. It was a simple fact. We would all die here because of him one way or another. So far, we had been fortunate. No one had been raped or killed---but it was only a matter of time. The rebels had spent some time with us and we knew how they operated.

Our parents made a hard decision.

"Bertha and I talked. She told me what the children said, and I do agree. It is no longer safe for me here and it is unfair to put all of your lives in danger. I will turn myself in at the G-2 office tomorrow. I will leave my fate with God."

This should have been a relief, but no one seemed relieved. Daddy's decision was likely a suicidal one. He was walking away to save us, but giving up his life in the process. By now, the fighters were no longer friendly.

"But why can't you run away? Just go somewhere else?" one of my cousins asked.

"I wish it were that easy, child."

"Why is it not? You can disguise yourself and leave."

"True, I could do that, but my face is well-known. If they caught me hiding, they'd certainly kill me and everyone with me. I can't live with that. I will go to them and pray the Lord finds favor on me."

With that settled, we agreed to have the two boys in the house take Daddy to the G-2 office via the swamp route. He would queue for rice at Tula Dennis' house like everyone else who came for rations. He was certain the rebels would grab him from the line. The rest was up to Higher Beings. Our boys escorted Daddy as far as they could and returned home.

Disturbing News

"Bertha, the way I saw them beating Mr. Azango with the gun on his head, hmm, I don't know if he would live, oh."

"Hmm"

"I say, they got him in the sun, tied up, and they are just knocking his head and kicking him all over. If he survives this, then God really wants him to live."

My mother was a strong woman. I drew many things from her. But what I saw in her after that man's visit shook me. It was not that she gave up; it just hardened her in one way and broke her in a million other ways. If any relief was there, it was that we were not forced to watch this, as we had to do on the first day Daddy was beaten. Mommy refused to leave her husband, despite all he had put her through. She risked her life sticking around---just to take care of him. Mommy was the kind of woman who placed herself after everyone else. She was not going to bail out on her vows or her husband. But that day, I saw my mom in a broken state. She was as if dead but alive.

That day, when they released Daddy, we packed lightly and sneaked out of the compound. Just as we hit the fence, one of the rebel groups met us.

"Halt! Advance to be recognized!"

I nearly peed on myself when I heard those words.

"Weh play your going at this kina time?" the one in charge asked when we reached them.

"We going to our ollor family hus in DuPort road," Mommy ventured. "We nah geh food here and my children hungry"

"Dah lie chief, dey escaping," another injected.

"I am not lying. We have no more food, no medicine, my husband is sick and we can't even treat him. So what should I do, just sit here and watch my children starve and my husband die?"

"Oldma, don't worry, we will protect you. We are freedom fighters. We are not here to harm your but it is late and your can't travel. Imagine if my boss sees your traveling like this? I will be in big trouble. If you go like this, then it means we can't protect your. So your go back home. Tomorrow, I will send someone to help you."

Thus, we returned. However, I had no doubt Mommy was determined to leave.

A while later, that very night, we all fled to ELWA hospital where people were seeking refuge. There were no rooms available for latecomers, so we perched like the rest.

This relief was temporary. Not long after we arrived, the hospital was attacked. Rebel forces launched several rockets, effectively scattering those gathered. Even the sick who could move fled. We had nowhere else to go, considering who Daddy was. We decided to return to the house at GSA. We spent a night, nothing more.

We were under no illusions that we would ever be safe there. Early the next morning, we went to our Aunt Mabel Yealu's place, on the same GSA road. She and her children had not left the area; they gladly took us in their home. Under that roof were about seven children from three families and several more adults.

As anticipated, the rebels removed Daddy from the line and took him into greater Liberia. We did not hear from Daddy again until we left.

Breast Feeding

During the civil war, I breastfed my son and three other babies, because stores and businesses were closed. This was during the heat of the war, and everybody who could flee, fled for one reason or another.

The first child I nursed was one of my cousin's daughter, who was nearly a year older then my son. His mother would cut half of whatever food we found to eat that day, be it palm cabbage, wild roots or palm kernels, and add it to my food so that I could have enough milk to feed both children.

When the ECOMOG arrived in August, accompanied by the Independent National Patriotic Front of Liberia, (INPFL), a breakaway faction of the National Patriotic Front of Liberia (NPFL), they swept our area and set up camp in homes all around the city. Many people were unsure of what to expect from the foreign forces, but they figured they could not be worse than the AFL or the rebels. Or so people believed.

We remained on alert, expecting the unexpected.

Human Shields

Later that night, as we tried to settle in with our new 'protectors', we heard them.

"Weh ley dam pepo dah living here? Yor geh ley hell orsah nah!"

Any apprehension we had was just justified. The rebels were back.

"Single file, anyballay nah in de line wey die! Allor yor dah dam enemy connapers. Yor think dah peacekeepers wey protect yor? We come here to protect yor bor yor nah lek good. Any dog dah wey try me toneh, I weh skin dem. Stupid pepo."

Our neighbors stood in line. I don't think anyone was sleepy anymore. We had seen how the rebels would stand on one side of the line and open fire. Anyone slightly out of line would be hit. Immediately, the people lined up single file. These rebels knew how to grab one's attention; they did not need subtlety.

Everyone in the house just stood there, unsure what to

do. We had moved away from the windows by then. The rebels were one house away. They'd be here any time now. They entered our compound moments later; we still had not decided what to do. As they approached the main door, sporadic gunfire came from our left, away from where the rebels were lining up civilians.

The rebels halted their approach and returned fire. For the next hour, they fired back at whoever was attacking them. We civilians ran all over the place, many falling by stray bullets. We took to the floor and hugged it. Anything above a foot was fair game. We had to smoosh into the floor, wishing it to create a gap. If they continued this any longer, we would all perish. Several adults and children urinated and defecated on themselves. Bullets ripped through furniture, utensils, walls and doors, windows and wood. Nothing was spared. We just stayed there.

Then, just like that, the shooting stopped. No warning, no breaking, from chaos to silence. The forces attacking stopped firing. The rebels took the reprieve to leave. We felt this was our opportunity to flee, so we all came outside. As we gauged our bearings, we had to figure out which way to go. The trick was, we had to ensure we did not run into either the rebel forces nor their counterparts, the ECOMOG. Right now, we did not know which to trust.

Bang!

Blaaaaaash!

Booooom!

The house down our lane exploded, freezing everyone

where they stood. Moments later, another, much closer, went up in flames. Almost immediately after that rocket landed, another followed. This one hit one part of our house, falling mostly on the road. We needed no warning. This time, we were certain what we needed to do.

Everybody ran---most just as they were. Some people grabbed on to items they had taken out of the house. I dropped my emergency bag and grabbed my son and ran. I ran anywhere I saw space, away from where the rockets were coming from. I didn't look back or sideways. I didn't think about friends or family. I just ran. My mind processed one instruction dangerously loud: "RUN!"

Behind me, unknown to me, my family members were running as well. By the time I stopped a good distance away from our house, I was breathless. The rest of the family was there. "Thank goodness," I thought.

We began taking stock. It seemed we were all accounted for. But then: "Musu, where is your baby?" my aunt asked my cousin. She looked towards me. I had been breastfeeding the baby before the shooting started. The baby had been sleeping, that much I recalled. We all turned to Musu; she kept staring at me. I returned her stare innocently as she looked my way.

"The baby is....."

Boom! Another rocket dropped---this time close to us. It drowned out her words but I knew then that she'd left the baby in the house.

"Run, yor leh go, dey coming, oh" someone from around

the corner of the next house shouted. We all set into action. But my aunt had that look. She said "Musu, you can't leave the baby there."

"Aunty, I can always have another..."

Boom. Boom. Boom.

Everyone took off. I ran back towards the house. I heard my aunt yelling something at me but I wasn't thinking---at least not in the terms of full processing. My instinct had taken over. I had a connection to that child; there was no way I was leaving the baby there. No one tried to stop me, at least I don't think they did, since the next thing I recalled was scurrying through the rubbish of the house searching for the baby. Bombs were still falling, shots were still being fired, and stray bullets flew all over the darn place. Yet, my mind had one goal: find the baby.

The baby was quite helpful in this regard. For, faintly among all that clatter, I heard the distinct cry of a baby--- a wailing baby. The mattress was a secret location we hid the kids under, in case they suddenly felt an urge to cry; it was muffling most of the sound. I grabbed the baby. I didn't check for anything. If it could cry, it was alive. I ran out right back toward the direction I had come from moments ago.

Surprisingly, as I neared the area, I heard my name. My people had refused to leave without me. They were hiding under anything offering some protection, awaiting my return.

The mother grabbed hold of her baby. I took my son, and away we went. It was no big deal what I did. It was what needed to be done. I recall how, later on, they kept saying I was brave, fearless and even heroic. I felt none of those things. A child I took as mine was in grave danger. I acted as any mother would. It is that simple.

We fled to Barnesville, Somalia Drive, to our other relatives' place in Logan Town, Bushrod Island ,for refuge. A week later, my mother and I left the rest of the family in search of her lost cousin. Mommy had been worried about her; then we heard that she was back home. There I found two other children who needed milk. When my mother pleaded with me, I ended up breastfeeding those little boys. She had gone blabbering that I had enough milk in my breasts, that I had even helped a child in Paynesville.

One of the boys was the child of my cousin, while the other boy's mother gave birth in the house and ran away, abandoning her malnourished child.

In all, I had three children to breastfeed, including my son, who used to sleep with the breast in his mouth. He drank excessively. This often left me weak with hunger. Many mornings I was so faint, I could hardly stand.

Sadly, only two of the kids I nursed are alive---my son and the first little girl. The two boys I breastfed at my cousin's house died later.

Dead Body Bone

Interestingly, the new batch of rebels had new sets of rules. A peculiar one was how they named children. The majority of them carried around AK-47 rifles, whilst the rest had Berettas. For some reason, the rebels had taken to naming newborn babies after their guns. The boys they called AK-47s and the girls, Berettas. Thus, when I gave birth, the rebels came to our house the next morning.

"Weh ley new baby ma eh?"

"Yeah," I said dryly

"Weh chah you geh?"

"Dah boy."

"Okay, hay name da AK-47. Anytime we come here da ley name we wan hear. "

"Hmmm." I was mad, but what choice did I have?

"You nah wan tor? If you nah call dis baby AK-47, we way kay you."

"Okay," was all I could manage.

From then on, they would make it a point to drop by often and ask after their 'son.' "Babyma, weh AK?"

"He insah."

"Good. Here two cup of rice. We bring ay for you to ee and fee ley baby."

"Okay, thank you."

"You mon nah gay ley food to ollor pepo oh. Eee ley and make ley baby fat. He fine" he offered, to my surprise.

"Thank you."

"Now gellor from my face lemme go debedah some enemy dem."

Just like that, he rushed off. Life and death always swung on a pendulum by a thin thread during the war. It took little or no provoking for life to be extinguished or death to be visited.

Do you remember how I said the rebels used to come to our place for animals and other valuables? My aunt never liked this. She did everything to stay away from them, as well as to keep us away from the rebels.

Many times, they would try joking with us. A few times, some of them would actually pass by to 'check on us'. We did not have much of a choice. Aunt used to say: "Too much familiarity breeds contempt." We often brushed it aside; not all the rebels seemed fearsome.

One fateful day, the strangest thing happened.

As we sat around, a rebel who often came by dropped in and began a serious lecture. He was called Dead Body Bone and he was fond of coming in to our yard and speaking Kpelleh to a girl living with us. He came that afternoon and said:

"Doggit, since dis morni my gun nahn eat nahthing yet."

"Weh you mean, ay nahn eat anything. Gun can eat?"

"Looka dis fooley geh. Ay can eee."

"Wetting ay can eee?"

"Human being; ay gapping I so I need to kill something quick." Immediately, he stood up, looking around. Then he approached me, and grabbed my son, whom I was breastfeeding, from my lap. He lifted the baby by one leg and then hung him upside down and shouted: "This is a Krahn baby, so I will kill him." I was dumbfounded, yet I jumped to my feet. I was unsure what to do or say. I was conscious that a wrong move could end my child's life. He would hit the floor before I even reached him.

Right away, the girl shouted in Kpelleh, and said, "This is my brother's baby, so if you kill him you have killed a Kpelleh child." Upon hearing those words, he lowered the baby and threw him at the girl. He left without a word.

7

LOVE AFFAIRS

Love Matters

"Hello, sweetheart."

"Yes, my love, how are you?"

"All is well. I have missed you so much."

"You think you have, but I have missed you more. I couldn't sleep last night."

"Don't worry, everything will soon be fine."

"I love you."

"I love you, too."

Like most adolescents, I believed I was in love. I was going out with a young man, Sammie, who was a few years older than I was. He read mathematics at the University of Liberia. He was also a part-time teacher at a public high school. I guess this made him to appear somewhat cool to me. I mean a young guy, good with numbers, smart, sexy and a smooth talker---what girl could resist?

I used to hang on his every word at times, and he certainly had an opinion or two. Being opinionated myself, it was not hard to see why we stuck it out. We could discuss many things and never tire of conversation.

Ours was a match made in heaven. We had all the trappings of romanticism, and had to deal with just enough reality to tear ourselves apart and go to our own homes, only to get back together the next day and start anew. No one could say anything to me that would cause me to leave the love of my life. Life could not be any better. Or could it?

Sammie was a typical lover boy. He was a super charmer, smooth talker and knew how to make a girl's heart melt. He had stolen mine, wrapped it and packaged it in some freezer; at least it felt that way.

By now, we had had a million ceasefires in our country, none of which seemed to hold long enough. Mommy was diabetic and finding it increasingly difficult to get the treatment she needed in Liberia, so she left for the US.

I was home all alone and enjoying every bit of it. I had a whole house to myself. The boys who stayed with us remained, but it was clear I ran the show. I wasn't unsupervised though; my Aunt Grace Morris gave me monthly allowance from rent collected on Mommy's behalf. She watched over me.

I took full advantage of the opportunity to allow my boyfriend to spend the weekends whenever he wished. Over time, he practically moved in with us. After all, love does matter.

Abuse Matters

Life was sweet until---it wasn't any longer. A cancer had erupted and I, knowing not the better, was equally guilty for fostering it. I groomed a monster that grew up to consume me.

Whenever Sam and I went out and other boys looked at me, he would squeeze my hand tightly or pull me closer to him. I must admit, to a young maiden, this sign of jealousy was appealing. What I did not know was that I was feeding a beast. His little possessive attitudes soon became annoying, then dangerous, then nearly lethal.

He went from pushes and shoves, to slaps and punches, and then kicks to merciless beatings. It didn't matter if I spoke to a boy or shook a hand. It didn't matter if it were real or imagined. It just existed and compressed me into a box I had no control over.

There was this one time I went to a friend's party. As we sat drinking and chatting, he barged in, "What are you doing here with all these boys around you?"

I was embarrassed, and tried to pass off a joke just to save face. "Oh, but you know all these guys, what could they be doing? I am just partying."

"Oh, so you think you cheeky, ehn?"

"I am not *cheeking* you up."

"You want make me shame in front of people?"

"I nah making you shame."

"So na, you torking back?"

"I ...." A slap came out of nowhere. It was warm, even hot, and had me seeing stars and constellations. I froze. Imagine the embarrassment! I'm not sure I even felt the pain. Whilst reeling from the slap, he grabbed me by the hair. I had recently got some hair extensions. He had handfuls of the hair at each grab---pulling and twisting. He practically dragged me out of the place by my hair. The best option, I felt, was to go along. At least by not resisting, I saved myself enormous amount of pain from his hair pulling, or even worse, having large chunks of my hair pulled out.

"Ay Sam, dah me you disgracing like this?"

"You nah see disgrace yet, wait let's reach home. When I fini way you, you wey know disgrace!"

"Bor whetting I didn't do anything wrong so why?"

"You will know why, jeh keep talking."

"Bor you herting me and you nah wan me to tork? Stop ay oh."

"You belleh shullor your dam muf ehn!"

"Ay Gor, my pepo dey man herting me."

"You nah see nothing yeh. Foolish geh. Come be hanging around dese smor smor boys dem. I'd rather kill you dan see another man have you." Then he walked away into the other room, leaving me in pain.

This was the first time he had publicly assaulted me, at least overtly. Everything before was building up to this point. At home, he used to slap me and drop a few punches. A few times, I got kicked and elbowed, ending up with blue and black eyes. Each time, I felt I needed to do better and stop angering him. He had a short fuse, so it was on me to stop igniting it. He made me feel like I was the one who was wrong. He drummed in my head that he loved me and did not wish to hurt me but could not control his anger. As long as I did not provoke him, we would be just fine.

I took him back every time. Initially, I was all for saving my love. I needed to keep my first love. "Who else would love me and my child as he did?" I wondered. I resolved to 'do as he said' just to improve

65

things. I accepted my bullheadedness. I figured this was the root of our problems. I knew I should not be talking back, even when I did not agree with him. I could let it go for the sake of peace.

The trap that most abuse victims fall into, I fell there and worse; I lived there. I made myself believe that by following him, things would improve and the abuse would stop.

The next morning, I reported him to my Aunt Grace Baker Morris. She was so angry, she had him arrested and detained. Immediately after she left the police depot for work, I went there, dropped all charges, and had him released. It seemed that my aunt didn't understand the magnitude of things. If she pushed this further, I could lose my love. He'd rot in prison. That I could not allow to happen.

When she returned from work, she passed by the police depot only to find out that he had been released. I'd never seen Aunt Grace so angry, apart from when we'd told her about the attempted rape over a decade ago.

"Mae, what's this nonsense I am hearing that you freed that fool?"

"Yeah, I did. He promised never to do it again and said that we could fix our problems like adults."

"Adults? The boy is a weakling to be hitting on a woman. He ain't fit to be called a man, much less an adult!"

"But the police were talking about prosecution and prison. I didn't want him to go to jail. I just wanted you to talk to him and teach him a lesson small.

"Mae, my child, ain't no talking to people like that. They don't understand that language. You prosecute and jail them. Simple. They can't change."

"Teta Grace, I beg you. I love this man, and if you want to help me, just talk to him. I am sure he will listen if you tell him. He already promised me never to hurt me again."

We argued bitterly. Neither of us could see things as the other did, so we ended up with my aunt promising never to interfere in our affairs again.

Things were fine. He was the model man, dazzling me with presents and even smoother talk. I was an eggshell. He was the tender handler. Life was never better. I knew that I did the right thing by giving us another shot at things. We'd just had a rough patch. People do change. Here was proof.

Not long after our blissful period, he beat me. This time, he even tore off my clothes, pulled me by my hair and dragged me like a rag. He said to me, "Let's see

67

who will come to your rescue this time. Your aunt has washed her hands of you. I will beat you like one market dog." I had run out of options. It was just not in me to submit blindly. Submission is not a problem, but I must understand the reason why, and this made no sense. People around me all left me alone. I could run to no one close---in or out of the family. He had successfully isolated me.

The beating was demeaning. It debased me so much I felt nearly worthless. Nothing angered me more. I had much to offer, so why was this boy-of-a-man desperate to show otherwise? I got fed up this time and went to the police after he left the house. Later, when he returned, I had him arrested for assault. He thought he could sweet-talk me into freeing him as I did the first time.

He tried, oh, he did. But I knew that I had to do this and do it right then. If I did not, I would spend the rest of my life condoning this violation of my being.

The police solidified my resolve when, for a minute, I considered releasing him and just letting him go. They said if I agreed to free him, I should write a note to say that if I died---since he'd threatened to kill me---the police were not to be held responsible. I knew that no one deserved that much power over me but me. I am unsure even I deserve that power. I refused his entreaties and left him there.

Everything Matters

It is usually said that when children from abusive homes see their fathers beat their mothers, they grow up thinking it is the norm. However, that was not applicable in my case. My father never once laid a finger on Mommy. I had no experience from home to justify my own abuse.

I learned this from outside. Growing up, I had this burning desire to please and fit in with my friends. I was often the smaller one in class, and I desperately wished to be one of the 'big girls.' I joined their clique and heard things I was too young to know. I then started trying those things, so that I, too, would have stories to tell. The more they told and teased me, the more I proposed to act.

I acted once---and lost my virginity. Little did I know that I was losing more than just that; I was walking around pregnant. The experience that should have been pleasurable was miserably painful, dry, and unromantic. I had done it. I had something to tell and carry, unknown to myself.

I fell victim to peer pressure and each time they pushed or suggested, I jumped in head-first. The only time I found it in me to reject something was when they suggested that I terminate the pregnancy.

After we tried the wait-and-see approach and found out that this baby did not intend to go anywhere, I panicked. I just could not have this baby. My parents would kill me before anything else happened, or so I believed. I went back to my trusted girlfriend advisers and they offered me some potion. I found out it contained several strong detergents and other chemicals culled from pantries. I was supposed to drink it, and pray for the best.

I refused, but not because I was brave. In fact, it was quite the opposite. I was scared shitless. I feared that mixture was my sure ticket to the underworld. I figured life with a child could not be that bad. The news that one of our colleagues had died just recently, supposedly because she had tried one of these potions, was reason enough to harden my resolve.

So I went home and never drank the potion. I also realized I did not have to do crazy things to fit in. I learned the hard way. Today, I have a handsome and intelligent young man I would have lost if I had made that choice my friends recommended.

Oh, and my parents did not kill me, either.

8

MORE SHENAIGANS

By my late teens, all my siblings had left the house. They were studying in the US. Mommy felt I needed a companion, so she brought in a girl, Helen, to live with us. Whenever Mommy traveled, she left us with Aunt Grace, who had her own three girls. Jocille Morris was much older, but my cousins Junda and Vivian were about age mates. We made up the four musketeers. Crazy is the only word needed to describe the bunch. We were always up to some kind of mischief.

This one time, when Teta Grace left for work, we collected some X-rated movies. We were watching until the lights went out. Now, we had one of those old VCR video decks. It held on to the cassette until it was powered back on, at which time it continued playing or restarted, depending on the model. We had only one, which was the main form of entertainment for everybody in the house.

We now had a crisis. It was almost time for our aunt to return home from work. She'd definitely be expecting to watch some movies before retiring for the day. We had to get the cassette out, and that we could not do just anywhere. People would wonder why young fresh girls like us were watching porn, something highly frowned-upon in our society. If a boy any of us dated found out, we risked looking desperate. If a guy we did not date saw it, we looked even more desperate. If an adult saw it, we would be completely finished. After much distress, we found a neighbor who allowed us to use the power to turn on the deck and remove the cassette. As soon as we replaced the deck back on its stand, Aunty Grace came home. We all burst out laughing. She thought us foolish, but we had the laugh of our lives at her expanse. If only she knew.

Exploring or Experimenting?

In my early twenties, I was no longer naïve to the likes of Sam. Remember the dude who flogged me? Long before I left him in jail, our drift apart began. He was then teaching mathematics at two different high schools. This provided him the opportunity to find himself some fresh girls.

He had taken to coming home quite late. That is, when he came home at all. We discussed it but little changed. One day, I asked him about something I had been hearing. "Sammie, I heard from one of your students that you have been loving to some of your students? Is that true?"

"Nonsense! Why would I do that? Why would I do such? Don't you know I could get in trouble for that?"

He had a point, but I just did not trust him. Since I had not caught him with anyone, I let it rest. But I kept observing him. By now, our sex life was nonexistent. He was so sneaky. He came home irregularly. The days he did, he was too tired to even stay up and talk for five minutes.

"Why do you drop right in bed as soon as you get home?"

"I can be tired. It is not easy teaching at two schools."

"I am not saying it is, but what has changed? I mean, was this not the same job you have always been doing? You even were going to lectures at the UL campus on top of that."

I got increasingly lonely. Matters were worse because he had isolated me. And he'd gotten me hooked on sex. Now, I was left in the cold with all those hormones, feeling insecure and lost. Despite my best efforts, nothing seemed to be changing. I got more reports about his infidelity. By now, I was no longer turning deaf ears to them. I needed to know for certain, if for nothing more than to move on with my life.

One night when he came home, I decided to confront him. "Sam, what is going on? You know that we are drifting apart, right? We don't talk, we don't go out together, we don't even make love anymore. Whenever we do, it is just mechanical."

"What are you complaining about again? Ehn sex dah sex?"

"Seriously? So dah today sex dah sex?"

"Mae, when I get home, I am often tired and do not want to make love. But you don't get that. I have told you before, please don't trouble me at those times. I only wish to rest."

This attitude went on for more than two months. I grew more convinced something was up with him. To imagine that when we began this relationship, he made me accustomed to having sex. Even when I was tired and refused him, he would prevail upon me and have his way. It was just something he did. He would be like: "Mae, you know that I love you dearly."

"But Sammie, I am tired and do not feel like having sex."

"What do you expect me to do now? I am horny and unable to control myself. You are the only one I love. If you refuse me, where do you expect me to get it from?"

"I am not refusing, but I am not in the mood. Every other time, don't I give it to you?"

"Yeah, but this is not every other time. I want it. I need it now."

"Baby, just wait. Tomorrow."

"Tomorrow too far. Look at me now; do I look like I can wait tomorrow? I don't blame you. I love you." He would later apologize and tell me how he loved me and could not control himself. I never really knew what to make of the whole thing. Thus, one can imagine my confusion over this new attitude.

Tired with hanging out in the cold, I soon began paying attention to a particular family friend, Champ. He had recently returned from the States. Since most of our friends had left the area, he stuck by the few, including me, who were still around. With time, his affection for me became clear. His interest grew, and he always stood near, comforting me and telling me the things I needed to hear. He treated me nicely and missed no opportunity to let me know that Sam did not deserve me. He fought for my heart, which he eventually won.

I guess the straw that broke the camels' back for me with Sammie was when my cousin, who attended one of the schools where Sam taught, informed me that he had impregnated a girl. Further digging revealed that it was not just one but two girls who carried pregnancies for him. It pained me that this same Sam had insisted that we not have children because I already had one. The idea that he could have two outside of our relationship was just too much for me. It seemed clear he just was not ready to be with me. It made Champ even more attractive. "Which girl turns down a gentleman for what I was stuck with?" At least I thought so.

Since Sammie was set in his routine, it left me with plenty time to catch up on my new love. You know how new love is sweet, right? We used up every ounce of the time Sam was away. I soon found it easy to replace him with Champ. Thus, wherever Sammie stayed out late, I would go seeking comfort in Champ's arms. I was exploring, as any young girl would be.

One fateful night when Champ was walking me home from his house, we did not know Sammie was creeping behind us. Champ walked me to my gate and was about to kiss me. Sammie immediately came between us and parted us with his hands. "I am Sammie and this is my girlfriend. Thanks for walking her. Please leave and go home." Immediately, he grabbed me by the hand and hauled me behind him. You don't have to guess what happened that night.

Winning or Losing?

The beating pushed me closer to Champ, who was enraged and wanted to confront Sammie. But I did not need that drama. It, however, sobered Sam up some. Sometime during that time, he confessed to the pregnancies and promised to be better. He was desperate to get me back. I was determined to be with Champ. I had no idea how it would play out.

Sam eventually began to show renewed interest and managed to convince me of his sincerity. I agreed to leave Champ. The problem was, how could I do it? Each time I went over to his place to break up, we made up.

Sam pleaded and made me promise; I foolishly agreed. Sam stayed away for two whole days. I did not see Champ for all that time. I planned to surprise Sam and break up with Champ. I wanted to do it when Sam came home. I did not know it would take him two whole days to return. Tired of waiting, I went over to Champ's. I took a friend along, to ensure I would do it.

We had a great time and forgot about ourselves. By the time we realized how long we'd been at Champ's, it was late, so Champ suggested we sleep over in the guest room. It was unsafe for two women to travel late during those times. Thus, we settled in for the night.

Sam had come home, and discovered I was out. He tracked me to Champ's place. He stood at the window listening. He did not have to wait long to hear me blare out one of my loud laughs. He assumed we were having another kind of great time so he banged on the window. "Come outside, Mae. I know you are in there because I heard you laughing." The laughter stopped and the entire place turned quiet. No one did or said anything. A few minutes later, Sammie shouted again, this time with a threat: "Champ, please put my woman outside or at the count of five, I will break down your door." Sure enough, when he finished counting, he started breaking down Champ's door.

Champ, raging with equal anger, took his father's AK-47 rifle and shouted from behind the closed door: "Sammie, if you do not stop banging on my door, I will blow your damn brains out and I will not be punished because you are a trespasser in my yard." Champ advanced the rifle, with his hand on the trigger. I stood in front of the gun; his adopted brother joined me. We begged him to calm down. When Champ's brother finally succeeded in taking the gun from him, Sammie started shouting at the top of his voice: "My people yor come ohoo. Champ wants to kill me for my woman business."

In order not to create further chaos, my friend and I left with Sammie. By the time day broke, news of two men fighting over me spread like wild fire. It was the hottest news on GSA road.

Eighth Floor, Where Things Happen

In all the confusion, I found a strange kind of solace on the Eighth Floor. There I continued to explore and mingle with people who tested my resolve and my morals. I eventually used the Eighth Floor to recalibrate my life. This was not intentional I guess, but, in hindsight, it becomes clear that events at that place helped reset my moral and social compass back to normal.

"Mae do not always be in the position to say: 'Do you see what has happened to me again?' Instead, you should make things happen." Those were the exact words of my neighbor living on the Eighth Floor, where all sort of things happened. Some things that happened were girlfriends booking their boyfriends with other women, and boyfriends jumping from upstairs to the ground to flee the scene.

It was a place where all rules of decorum were suspended. People often went there in search of their missing spouses. On the Eighth Floor, anything went. The tenants of the building developed a reputation over time that was both fearsome and abhorrent. This was the big league, and I so wanted something different, I was willing to try it.

I guess I never saw it in terms of wrong and right. It was more like living on the edge; being on top of things; making change. In reality, when all the drama was over, the people inside were the ones whose lives were being damaged, affected or changed forever---and not necessarily for the better. The time it took to realize this was short, but for some the damage was irreparable.

I can remember one night, a married man came looking for his wife. He'd heard that she frequented the place. He said in a disturbing voice: "My man, I am surprised at you. I hear my wife is here."

But my neighbor said: "My man, she is not here; you can come see for yourself." He had smuggled her over the balcony to the other apartment where I lived and she fled the area, while her husband went inside to search. That was just a tip of how things went down on the Eighth Floor, where things happened. I guess this was a reality check for me.

Dismantling or Unravelling?

However, my world was about to change and I had no clue. One day in 1996, during the ULIMO-J war, we fled our house for DuPort Road because the fighters were breaking into government officials' houses. I happened to meet a long lost friend in the market, who had just fled her home in Sinkor. "Hey dear, how you been? It has been so long. Where have you been?"

"Mae, what are you still doing here? I thought you left this place long time, you girl."

"Leave? What are you talking about? We are still here, as you can see."

"I do, which is my worry."

"Where do I know besides here?"

"So you think dah joke, ehn?"

"I told you before you left the last time..."

"Chay!"

"I ain't know what? You are confusing me girl. What are you talking about?"

"Oh, you haven't heard?"

"Heard what? You're scaring me."

"Oh, you need to be scared. I myself who here, I scare for you. You belleh be scare."

"Okay, stop all the games and tell me what you are hinting at. Wetting I nah do for me to be scared?"

"So you mean you really don't know? Oh my God!"

Now, I was beyond confused. We were in the midst of the war and everything mattered. Even a wrong perception, look, or sneer could be fatal.

"Mae, dah your old jue, Sam, dah big freedom fighter, oh. He some kahn nah big commander with Taylor's rebel. I saw him the ollor time and he say he wor coming for you. I nah ley only one who wor der."

"What?"

"Yes, I swear!"

"Gbah stop this kindna joke."

"I nah joking. Ask anybody from the area. The man is seriously coming for you."

"Oh, you serious?"

"Gbah how will I joke about something like that? The man saw us in the line. He made allor us from the area to pass and told us he was coming back for you. He said that the last time you refused to go with him so he is coming with his gun and nothing or nobody would stop him."

9

EXILE UNREALITY

Fleeing the Familiar

I heeded that warning and I took my six-year-old son and escaped with my childhood friend and her family to Ivory Coast. While in Cote D'Ivoire, we lived worse than second-class citizens did. There were no refugee camps. Refugees were restricted to the region closer to the border. Danane and Man were the key spots for Liberians. Then there was Abidjan.

When we were newly arrived, we had to face culture shock. Many strange things happened. One time whilst in the market, I saw a man spit in the face of another woman who had mistakenly bumped into him. Whilst she wiped away the mess, he said, "Chien la."

We had to rent from locals. This was particularly difficult. Most of us had come from Monrovia and other main cities.

These locals were in the heart of the interior. This pitted the two lifestyles against each other. It was easy to see why some locals believed we were extravagant and wasteful.

Soon, the cost of living began going up. Being city dwellers, many were accustomed to paying rent at amounts far higher than anything these new landlords ever imagined receiving.

Thus, when they quoted low rates, some of us paid for a year or two, simply securing their lodging, since they did not wish to be put in the street one day if they did not have money for rent. Refugees had no source of income, so people were trying to be smart about their choices and finances.

The locals took this otherwise. It appeared to them that refugees had money, so they were fair game. Some refugees were evicted and the balance of their rent returned if another refugee offered more money for a place. This bidding translated into higher prices for food and other services.

Another common phenomenon was having to deal with aggressive landlords. People could not easily get work, so refugees depended on relatives in the US or abroad generally for sustenance. This was not always forthcoming. These relations had to live as well. There were often delays. Some property owners were decent enough to understand; others were not so. They'd take matters into their hands. Some would seize the pot with food in it, demanding payment or the tenants would neither eat nor get back their utensils.

If a tenant took a case to the UNHCR, the landlords would appease them, and the tenants would be none the better. The truth was, there were way too many cases of a similar nature, most of which had amounted to naught.

I am aware that this is not representative of most Ivoirians. I can only speak to what I saw, experienced and know. I make no claim to judgment.

Unfamiliar People

The Francophone countries are hard to live in for someone from an Anglophone country because the language is another barrier. Cote D'Ivoire was not different from other Francophone countries. Living as a refugee, one had to be careful not to get into a problem with an Ivorian because getting into trouble often ended badly for the refugee. Life was not as dangerous as it was at home, obviously, but it was not much better for many who had no source of income and depended on handouts from the UNHCR, which was hardly a reliable means of support.

Familiar Culture

However, not everything was a hard swallow. Soon, we people began bridging the cultural gaps and discovered that we had familiar culture with the Ivoirians. Because we shared a common border, we intermarried. The Gio, Krahn and Grebo all had relatives in Ivory Coast. National borders were impositions by colonial masters, but relatives lived right on the other side of each other. There was only a little stretch of water dividing both nations at many parts. We eat almost the same food, and speak almost the same dialect in most parts along those rivers.

10

EVERYTHING ELSE

Punches and Blows

I returned home from exile in 2000. A year after, I enrolled in a one-year journalism program. This was when I met my daughter's father, Momolu, who swept me off my feet for the second time. In no time, I got pregnant. It was 2002. Six months into the pregnancy, my people insisted that he marry me. He promised to do so after I gave birth because my stomach was far too big to do a church wedding.

Three months after delivery, I told my man I wanted to find a news outlet and put into practice what I had learned.

"Momolu, I think the baby is big enough. I am considering finding work."

"What work?"

"Being a journalist, of course!"

"You are joking me, right? With this young baby, you seriously want to go and work for someone else?"

"Yes, you forget that I went to school for it. I had to miss my internship, so I need to get this job."

"What work? How much will they even pay you? Is it because of peanuts that you want to leave my child to go and do?"

"It is not about the money, I want to build my CV. I can't exactly put Baby Ma on it now, can I?"

"I see no reason for you to go working just yet. Stay home and take care of my baby."

"But I really need to do this. It will help me one day in the future. When my child is grown, what will my excuse be?"

"Well, maybe you can find work at that time."

"I don't think that is the best solution."

"What better work you are talking about? How much is that? $5? Okay, stay home and I'll pay you $50 to take care of my child; that is ten times over the peanuts they will give you."

My people called him again so that we could discuss the wedding, and he said we should go ahead with the plans. While waiting, I found a job as a scoop reporter in 2003 with the Telegraph Newspaper, a small, weekly paper, and I earned $500 Liberian dollars, far less than that five US dollar salary he mentioned. My man got angry. Eventually, he took every opportunity to denigrate my profession and my job. He did everything to keep me away from working.

I worked for two years with the Telegraph, and then moved on to the Daily Observer, which was a daily paper with a bigger audience than the Telegraph Newspaper. It was like a dream when I was told that my take-home salary was going to be $60 US dollars. Can you imagine what it was like for me, who was working for less than five dollars? I felt like I had hit the jackpot. Even though I eventually learned that many journalists made far more than that, I was still so happy at the same.

On the home front, things had not improved. In fact, Momolu and I were drifting on one of those slow sailing boats. Unfortunately, it seemed we each had a boat and no longer shared the same one.

When our child was nearly two years, I walked in one night and there was Momolu, kissing a girl. "What the hell are you doing? In our house, too?"

It was obvious they were expecting to be caught. But his response was even worse than I expected, "Whetting you see me doing?"

"Oh, you mean I did not see you two kissing?"

"It is no time for you to start that your thing here again, oh." He went about ranting until he turned hostile.

Things stayed tense between us when he started sleeping out more often. When I confronted him again one day regarding the lady, he said to me: "If you left your father's house to move into mine because you think I will marry you, you better think again. I am sorry, Mae, because nobody will force me into doing what my father could not get me to do when he was alive"

"What are you talking about? Who is forcing you to marry?"

"Answer that one yourself. But I'm not rush into anything."

"My family is not forcing you to do anything. We have a child; we are living together. You said you wanted to marry me; so where is the force?" I was taken aback by that comment more than by any of the other things he had done. I think that was the breaking point for me. It was never the same again. Each time, it felt like I was forcing myself on him and that I couldn't take.

After six months, I raised the issue of the baby and our safety. By then, he would leave us alone in a four-bedroom house and sleep out nearly every night. "You can't keep putting us in danger, Momolu. If you will not sleep here at least say so ahead of time.   Let me find a way to go home, or have someone sleep here. This house is too big for just the two of us to be in."

"I don't have time. It is the work. I never know when I will be home."

"That is a cheap excuse."

"That is no excuse. It is the truth."

At last, when I could not get him to agree to stop sleeping out, I suggested, "I think I should move back to my parents' house if this continues!"

"That is the best decision you have ever made. I am overwhelmed with work and would sleep out more often." With that said, he packed us up and sent us away to my parents' house in Paynesville.

After a week, I heard he'd moved her in with him, but I refused to believe it until I could confirm it personally.

One evening, I went unexpectedly to his house. I knocked,

and when he opened the door, he was shocked. As he stood in the doorway, blocking it, she called out from the bedroom we once shared: "Momolu, who is that at the door?"

"Nobody, dear."

"Oh, so I am now nobody?"

"You have been pushing me too long, Mae. I am tired."

"So, that is your excuse?"

"It's not an excuse, it is the truth."

"I made you do this?"

"Yes, you did."

"How? You went out, found a woman, brought her in our house and I met you kissing. Since then, you have changed, and each time I ask, you deny it. You move her in once we leave the house and I am responsible for that? How?"

"You have become too nagging. Always complaining."

"Okay, let me come inside. Let's talk."

"Go home and come tomorrow. If you are serious to talk, we will."

"Why should I go? I'm going nowhere. In fact, I will sleep here tonight."

He immediately said, with no remorse: "Is this not what you wanted to see? So you came here to cause trouble? You now want to sleep here at whatever cost? But if you think I will put her outside because of you, you better rethink. I would do no such thing. So if you know what I know, you better go into the guest room to pass the night and go home tomorrow morning."

If the ground could open, it would have swallowed me

because it was the biggest humiliation I had ever faced. Moreover, it came from the man I loved more than myself. I spiraled into a serious bout of depression. By the evening of the next day, less than twenty-four hours later, I was hospitalized. The shock was excessive.

At the Catholic Hospital emergency ward where I was taken, the doctor hurriedly inserted an IV into my veins, in order to relax my body and stop the reaction. After two hours of treatment and observation, he said it was shock that had rendered me into such a condition. We talked and when he found out the source of my anger, he gave me fatherly advice and said whenever I felt my veins locking in similar way, I should weep and not keep the hurt within. Weeping is not a sign of weakness, but helps release stress and tension as well.

By then, my friend called Momolu, who came to the hospital reluctantly. That night, when my treatment was over and I was discharged, he took me home ---only to go right back to his house with the other woman.

The next week, after not seeing him since my discharge, he came over. It was my birthday. I was hopeful he would spend the night and we would use that time to catch up and discuss this situation. He came quite late and we were in the room about to sleep, or so I thought. Then out of the blue he says: "Mae, I do not think that things can work between us. I do not love you again. I barely get aroused by you. I see you more like a sister."

"What the ...?" I thought.

As if the bugger read my mind, he said: "But during the time I am with my other woman, I am active. Doesn't this mean I am no longer in love? I think this is a sign. However, the child will be between us and I will still support my child."

A week ago, I thought he'd said the worst things, but right now he topped it. It was not just what he said, nor the way he said it. It was something else. If he could form this thought, entertain it, think the words and actually utter them, then we were indeed doomed, at least in his mind. A person could never feel that confident about trashing another's heart. No one should be that relaxed saying words that will tear another to their soul---not unless they meant it. Or if they were fed up with the other person and definitely wanted to cut that deep.

Thoughts. They assaulted me. I felt lost. I was treading down the same road of a week ago, only faster this time. The years of planning a wedding that would not be; the toils, the hardship, sacrifices, shame; you name it. Everything hit me, each competing for immediate attention. I was overloaded.

Rivers of tears flowed. I cried it all out. In between, I made one desperate effort to save us. Anything would go now. Through sobs, I said: "Well, since you say you do not want me, I will just become a prostitute and not be committed to any man again, because what is the use of living?"

He replied unexpectedly: "Well if that is the life you want, you can go ahead and I won't stop you."

"Seriously?

"But if you ask me, I would say you should think it over.

Whatever you decide won't change my mind."

"You came here to kill me, right?"

"You will kill yourself, not me. I am just saying how I feel. The truth."

"You picked my birthday, a week after you put me in the hospital, and do this to me?"

"I picked no day. I just wish to say the truth. I can't pretend any longer."

Those words confirmed my fears but they cut like hell. They went right to my soul. Ripped it to shreds and shredded the shreds. They didn't break me. They didn't tear me. They just stayed like needles stuck in an uncomfortable place, refusing to budge.

I continued: "Just a week ago, the doctor warned you against putting me through such tension that would result in to my death, but here you are breaking such news to me, when I am not fully recovered. You do not need to kill me before you carry on your relationship with your new-found love. You can go ahead, I will live."

I do not know where that courage came from, but I stood up, wiped my tears and told him words I had only thought of before this time. I spoke power into my situation. I was just a high school graduate with a year of basic journalism training. I had not enrolled into any college, but I challenged myself.

"I will not become useless, as you expect I would, but I will equip myself. I will educate myself so when you see me tomorrow, you will wonder how I got over it. This will not break me. This will not be the end of me. You watch and see. You have made the biggest mistake of your life. You will search for a woman like me, but won't find one. You could look for me but won't get me. You will one day want me back, but by then it will be too late for you." These words were spoken in confidence, as if I knew for a fact.

I now know that sometimes trials in our lives come about to make us strong and not to break us. They give us that determination which makes us forge ahead against all odds. If Momolu had not disappointed me, I would have been complacent bearing children and living with a man I was not married to. I would not have pushed on; I doubt I would have become what I am.

Fleeing the Clippers

On International Women's Day on March 8, 2012, I received an award when I reported a story on female genital cutting, (FGC) or female circumcision, (FC). When the story broke, my nine-year-old daughter and I went into hiding. The traditional people came looking for us to take us to Sande bush to have us circumcised. This was supposed to be punishment for writing about the taboo subject. Many people lashed out at me and said I was speaking against the culture and tradition of Liberia. I rejoined that I was simply trying to educate our traditional people against sending underage children to the Sande bush. The act of forced FC was a child's rights violation. I also wanted to highlight the medical implications of using unsterilized instruments. A story meant to educate nearly cost the lives of me and my daughter. We had to sleep in different homes every night. I had to live with the fear of not knowing if I'd survive the day or die and leave my daughter alone. What kind of messed-up existence is that? Even though many people were helpful to us---they took us in---those were only temporary fixes. None abated the threat to our lives. None calmed a mother who feared her child being taken to a Sande bush more than she feared for her own life. This was not about bravery. I was not being a hero. I was simply surviving.

Media Saga

In 2007, ten years ago, I was due to get married to one Tarnue Johnson, whom I met in the journalism school I attended after I returned from exile. He was kind and showered me with attention. With time, he won the girl.

We set a date for the wedding and I left for the US, where I was invited to a three-week media training with the Christian Science Monitor Newspaper in Boston, USA. While in the US, seven other reporters and I were invited to Providence, Rhode Island, to partake in a panel discussion and share our experiences as journalists in post-war Liberia. My topic was to speak about the challenges female journalists encounter in the line of work. I listed several common challenges: robbery, lack of funds, and sexual harassment.

I had the misfortune of encountering every one.

I was once approached by a newsmaker, a source for my former boss at the Telegraph Newspaper. We set up a meeting at an unassuming local bar, where he would turn over to me secret documents for my boss.

I met him at the location. He was drinking and already relaxed. When I took the seat next to him, he asked: "What are you taking?"

"A soft drink."

We engaged in light talk awaiting my order. He stared at me uncomfortably, but I made nothing out it. When my drink arrived and I was sipping, he leaned forward and said: "You know Mae, you are a beautiful woman."

"Thank you," I offered after a few moments of awkward silence.

"I am serious. You are one sexy chic. We could build a steady relationship. I give you documents, and in return, you jeh help ley papay warm hay fire smor. I am torking files da can make yor career." As he spoke, he took my free hand into his and began caressing it.

Shocked at his behavior, I pulled away, slammed the drink on the table and stood to leave. "I am not interested in making a name for myself that way."

"Why are you playing hard to get?"

"I didn't come here for that."

"Forget about that document business. Let's go have some fine time. We can do the story."

I immediately woke up, slammed the drink on the table, told him I was not interested and walked away without the documents.

"Mtweeeeeeeeeeeeee!" I hissed as I walked away.

"Oh, Mae, wait, let me bring the documents... he blabbered until I was out of earshot.

When I made that statement at that US conference, it caused a serious stir among some of my female counterparts. They dropped my language of sexual harassment and called it females selling their bodies for news. They drafted their own statement debunking mine. Yet, they agreed that males do attempt to, or actually molest, them during the course of their work. It soon became a war of words: harassment versus molestation.

As the controversy thickened, some accused me of seeking political asylum, hence my 'false' allegations.

By the weekend, the Ministry of Information, Culture and Tourism posted a press release on the Daily Observer Newspaper's website that Journalist, Mae Azango, was needed to face the Board of Inquisition at the Ministry upon her return to Liberia.

Sadly, my own paper, the Daily Observer, left me out to dry. In fact, when my boss, Mr. Kenneth Best, arrived in the US, he phoned me, suggesting that my statements had hung a dark cloud over his newspaper.

When I arrived home, nobody asked or ordered me to the

Information Ministry. I guess everybody was surprised I had returned home after being accused of trying to seek political asylum. Little did they know that a local press group already offered me a chance at asylum. They were willing to vouch for me if that was what it took but I refused.

The working relationship was no longer tolerable at my office. Many reporters avoided me. Sometimes, my stories were not published. At the end of the month, I resigned and was immediately employed by the Front Page Africa Newspaper. My new boss, Rodney Sieh, later told my brother: "Since Mae was disliked for speaking out the truth, we wanted her to work for us. We need someone who could speak out their mind and do so without fear."

Interestingly, the following year after the saga, some female journalists came up with a complaint to the PUL that female journalists were being sexually harassed by some of the their male counterparts, thus validating my claim

Wedding Palava

When I returned to Liberia in September 2007, we started preparations for the marriage to Tarnue. We sewed our clothes, got the rings, settled the food, drinks, musical sets and DJs. We even arranged for live performances. We expected to host approximately 1,000 people.

On the wedding day, Tarnue took the flower girl and ring bearer for their final rehearsal at the Hermon City Church on

DuPort Road in Paynesville, while my maid of honor and bridesmaids were getting me ready for the wedding. The wedding was set for one that afternoon. Around noon, I received a call from the pastor urgently requesting my presence at the church. When I arrived at the church, the pastor said, "My daughter, an unknown woman claiming to be Tarnue's wife called and warned me not to officiate at any wedding. She claims Tarnue is her husband. She didn't stop there, oh. She said that if we conducted any wedding between her husband and you, she was going to burn this church down along with everyone in it. So, the matter reach you nah."

Nothing in my dealings with Tarnue prepared me for this. This was simply out of character with the man I knew. Here I was, on my wedding day, but having to deal with the one thing any woman would dread on this day. I was actually in the church; the officiating ministers were there; the groom was there; most of our guests had arrived. We had all the ingredients for a wedding, but I had to consider the possibility of not getting married. This simply made no sense. It would be as bad as if Tarnue left me standing at the altar had he fled or had he reconsidered, or I if I were incapacitated. But we were all sound and healthy and as far as I knew, still in love. "So what the heck was this nonsense-woman talking about?" I wondered.

I don't recall how long it took me to process but the pastor had to break me out of my contemplation and bring me back to reality. "Child, weh you say?"

"The woman is lying!" Tarnue insisted. "She ran off with

98

another man and took my children. Even before that, only children business we had. She is somewhere there in Ghana, enjoying her life. Now she won come spoil my own."

Just then, the phone rang again. The pastor answered. He spoke for a while. "Yes I understand... Uh hmm... I know... Yes, I know... I see... Okay."

We all sat there. Tarnue kept protesting angrily, swearing and promising to get back at her if she ruined his happiness. I sat there, numb. Numb enough not to be able to process anything much anymore.

"Yes, she is here right now. Okay, hold on one minute." The pastor handed me the phone after informing me that the woman wished to speak to me. He wondered if I wanted to talk to her.

"Hello."

"If you ever want to enjoy your children, do not marry to my man, because I will kill you. I have suffered behind him too long that he has rendered me a handicap then you want to take him away from me? He can never leave me because we took an oath in blood that he will never leave me. So, it cannot happen, because I will kill you first before that can happen. I dare you to try me if I do not kill you, then I am not Taiwah from Guinea."

No pleasantries. Just raw facts. She was hurt, from the sound of her voice. I was less moved by the threats than the sound of her voice. Something about it told me she was not lying. She was speaking from a place of disappointment, one only a woman who has birthed children, then cleaned after and taken care of a man, can feel. No amount of love I had for Tarnue could erase the pain I now felt. I could understand her without having to try. I was once before like her, no, twice over. I could not now be that other woman who took away the man she loved.

Tarnue, on the other hand, was still denying ever being married to this woman. "She is lying, pastor. We only had children. We never married. We should not pay her any mind. Let's carry on with the wedding as planned."

After the telephone conversation, the pastor then sent his assistant to the lady's father, to confirm whether his daughter was ever married to Tarnue, since he insisted that the lady was lying.

When the assistant pastor and Tarnue got to the old man's house, the Oldman told Tarnue: "Look me in the face, son, and swear that I personally did not hand-deliver my daughter to your father, who had paid the bride price for my daughter."

Tarnue then said: "It was just a turnover ceremony of your daughter who was at the time pregnant, and not a marriage."

The old man shook his head in disappointment and said to Tarnue; "If you want to marry the civilize way to another woman, you can go ahead, but according to tradition, she will be your second wife. As far as I am concerned, my daughter is your first wife and you have never turned her over to me. If you do not want her again, you know what to do."

Upon relaying the message back to the two of us at the

church, the pastor concluded that he could no longer officiate at the wedding. "It puts me in a difficult spot, my child, but I can't break the law. Conducting this wedding without further investigation could be serious problem for us. I am so sorry."

My uncle Nyema Baker, who came to give me away, was astonished to hear the news and told me I shouldn't have a wedding at my place either, since it could turn into a bloodbath.

Later, we found out that the woman had paid some thugs from Red Light, who had hidden in the bushes with machetes and gallons of gasoline, with a direct order to kill the bride and burn down the church.

I took my uncle's advice and told the pastor to tell all the guests that the venue had changed to my house in Paynesville. When I disembarked from the vehicle that brought me there, everybody stopped and watched me--- many with eyes of disgust---as if I had committed a serious crime. I was the man-snatcher, the home-breaker and even the family destroyer. In those eyes were not questions, but accusations and judgments. No one likes the *other* woman, and here I was, flaunting her on my wedding day of all days.

It seemed foolish to me that any reasonable woman would think another woman would love to be or play the role of the *other woman*. Even if she did, would she do so on her wedding day? However, we had long passed that point. Judgment had already been rendered. I was guilty. Nothing I did or said here would change that for some of these very friends and loved ones. But I had to try, don't you think?

When I entered our house where the reception was to be held, I asked my brothers to call the guests in the hall. Without a tear in my eye, but loaded with emotions, I addressed them.

"Ladies and Gentlemen, thanks for leaving your busy schedules to come and celebrate with me, but I am so sorry to announce that the wedding is no longer taking place. The groom-to-be did not clean the mess from his own back yard before planning for a wedding. He said I should give him time to sort things out, but I am done, because when he had the time to sort things out, he was lying. There is enough food for all, so eat and drink. And to my friends in the media, you have your front-page story to carry on Monday morning. Since I have fixed my hair for a wedding which was not, I am going to attend Miss Liberia at the Unity Conference Center."

As I walked away from the crowd, my family people and friends were crying and rolling on the floor as if they were mourning someone's death. I consoled them and said: "If you cry, what do you expect me to do? However, if I am not crying from what happened to me, why should you cry? Wipe your tears, because God knows why this wedding did not take place."

A cousin and her husband came to comfort me. When they noticed I was under control, my cousin said: "Mae has everything under control. I came to console her, and she is consoling me instead." They left shortly before I left for the beauty pageant at the Unity Conference Center.

I did not shed tears because I said to myself that no man was worth my tears if he screwed up. In addition, if I had cried, I could have gone down the road of depression and grief, which could have ended worse. I knew all was not lost, and there was a future ahead. I stood firm because I could not afford to let my kids down.

Much later, Tarnue ended up moving in with Taiwah, the very woman he denied. They currently live together.

Dividing Kola

Some men can be shameless. Weeks after the aborted wedding, Mr. Tarnue Johnson came stepping to my house along with his best man seeking an audience with me. I agreed to see him despite everything. "Mae," he began, "I brought my best man as my witness to tell you that I have come for my wedding rings and the share of the gifts from the bridal shower, the share of the drinks that were not used at the reception, and the money the bridal party collected to purchase a gift for our wedding."

It took everything in me to stop from choking him. I could not begin to consider the depths one had to drop to before landing here.

"Not forgetting, my five thousand Liberian dollars I gave you the other time when I was begging you to accept me back," he interrupted.

Can you imagine a shameless man asking for dishes given as shower gift, and left-over drinks from a reception? He was brave to ask, when in fact, I did not seek anything from him for the waste of all the food and drinks my family provided.

Anyway, I managed to compose myself enough to say, "Tarnue, if you do not respect yourself and leave my yard, I will call my brothers to drag you out of here. You know how they are in wait for you."

"Aye, Tarnue!" his best man spoke. "I thought you said we came here to beg Mae to take you back? Mae, I'm sorry. I was led to believe we were coming to beg you, not do this." With that, he left the yard.

Suitor Wahala

Since my failed wedding, I refused to date anyone. I felt too raw to consider the idea. I resolved to heal before attempting any relationship.

However, that did not stop suitors from coming. It would appear that with each award I've bagged, there is no shortage of more. This has made my life somewhat cumbersome. I have had to scrutinize folks more than usual.

One shouldn't have to be a PI or detective before entering a relationship. This should be a normal process, right? One of my all-time favorite stories is about a professor, my suitor from Nigeria.

I met this Nigerian professor on-line. We dated virtually for a while. Eventually, he proposed marriage. This meant that I now had to go to Nigeria and determine the feasibility of this relationship.

From the day I entered Nigeria, to the day I left, the professor was all over me. He was possessive, aggressive and domineering. Matters were compounded, because I knew no one in the area. He lived well in the midst of the Boko Haram area north of Nigeria. Everyone I tried reaching out to back home reminded me to stay calm until I left his care. That was quite difficult to do, because of my nature. I had to pretend in order to survive.

One day whilst talking, I asked: "Why do you wish to marry me? I mean, there are many women, why me? How did you even get to know about me?"

He offered: "Do you know that I have been following you on the Internet for over two years? I watched you as you won all of your international awards. I then said to myself, I must get this lady at all costs, because she is well-known and will give me easy access to the international world."

Can you imagine a man telling a lady he is asking to marry him something like that? He did not end there. After I said I was not ready to marry him, he said, "Darling, even if you are not ready to marry me yet, just attach my surname to your surname. Let people address you as such, then the international people will start knowing me as your husband and will be willing to work or do business with me." I could not overcome my shock that any serious-minded person would do or say such.

"Oh, so you are only after me for fame?"

"Of course not, but you'd be my wife, wouldn't you? I will not be lying."

It amazed me when he further suggested, much later on in my stay, that I prostrate or kneel and bow my head in greeting him whenever he enters the house. This, he said, was his culture, and as his wife, I must obey. I have no issues with culture and tradition, but I find it hard to do a thing that belittles my person, reinforces a stereotype, or makes little sense to me. I did not see myself doing that and waiting upon my husband to be satisfied before I am relieved. So I asked: "If you are unhappy, then what do I do?"

"You'd remain there until I touch your head." I refused to believe that was required by tradition; even if it were, I was not settling for that. It seemed more like pseudo-slavery to me. I was not about to have another man take advantage of me---and this time, using culture.

REFLECTIONS

It's been a long road but worth every bit of it. Okay, maybe not every. I sure would have wished some things had turned out differently; and that some others did not happen at all. Yet, some things went just the way I had hoped. Moreover, if anything had been different, I might be a lesser version of me; that is unacceptable. I am here today because of all my experiences. All. I know it is nowhere near easy to break free from abuse and overcome hardship, but it can be done. I did. So can you. Many others did and are doing same, daily.

I wanted to bare it all: no gloves, no socks, no hats, no bra, just an open look into my closet. I wanted a girl somewhere, or a woman in another place, to see that their situations are not much different from mine. I did not need super powers to do it. I only needed to find myself deep under all that hate and anger. Once I found me, I began working on myself and my freedom. Freedom. It has been a most wonderful experience since I got it. It is not as glorious as made out. Many times, one wants to go back to the familiar, but with time and persistence, one gets the hang of it and then starts to enjoy it. No abuse is justified. Break that cycle. Break it NOW!

Epilogue

I left Liberia along with my 12 -year-old daughter Madasi, on the 26th of February, 2015, to attend and take part in the wedding of my God-sister in Texas, USA. It was exciting for both my daughter and me to travel together. By bad fortune, we did not arrive in the US until the 2nd of March, when the wedding was already over. That was tragedy beyond forgetting.

We were not allowed to board our connecting flight and our baggage was taken from the aircraft. Our passports and luggage were seized as if we were criminals. We were kept in a little room, along with other foreign nationals who had some problem with their papers and were also stopped from leaving detention in Morocco. We slept on the cold floor without any covers during very cold weather. They fed us a piece of bread and a bottle of coke every five or six hours. They told us to buy our own water, when there was no water sold in the place of detention. We did not bathe for days because there was no shower in the bathroom. Whenever we wanted to drink, my baby and I would have to go to the bathroom and drink from the bathroom faucet.

When I asked that our tickets be redirected to New York as we had US visas, they told me that my Godmother would have to buy a new set of tickets because we missed the flight. Did we do wrong to miss the flight when they took us off the flight? Then the immigration agent said he could not give back our bags, due to security reasons, and if a new set of tickets were not bought promptly, we were going to deported back to Liberia.

Luckily, for me, a girl from Nigeria came to detention. When she started communicating with her family members in Italy, I asked to use her phone for a minute to call the US.

We did not receive my bags from the airline for more than two weeks, so I had to buy everything we needed to wear during that winter. Did I say they are not paying me back for damage? Of course not.

ABOUT THE AUTHOR

Mae Azango is a multi-award winning Liberian journalist and female activist. She is known for her reports on female genital mutilation (FGM), which helped suspend the practice in Liberia. Azango is the daughter of Robert G.W. Azango, an Associate Justice of the Supreme Court of Liberia who was dragged and beaten by rebels, later dying from his injuries.

Mae Azango later became a refugee. She returned to Liberia in 2002 and began work as a journalist. https://en.wikipedia.org/wiki/Mae_Azango - cite_note-CPJ-3 Topics of her reporting included abortion, illegal mining, rape, teen pregnancy.

Ms. Azango is a recipient of the International Press Freedom Award of the Committee to Protect Journalists.

In 2011, Azango won a grant from the US-based Pulitzer Center on Crisis Reporting for her work on "under-reported stories" in "human interest and developmental journalism".

She lives in Liberia where she continues to advocate for female and child rights.

www.ingramcontent.com/pod-product-compliance
Lightning Source LLC
Chambersburg PA
CBHW071132090426
42736CB00012B/2097